ଓଃ

THE RAPOETRY OF A HUSTLER

BY

KAREEM TORAIN

Published by:
LOCK THE GLOBE PUBLISHING
P.O. Box 23639
Philadelphia, PA 1914-3

ISBN: 978-0-692-28080-5

Library of Congress Catalog Card No.

Rapoetry Of A Hustler
Poems by Kareem "K-Gotti" Torain
Written by Kareem "K-Gotti" Torain
Graphic Design by Clash Graphic Flyers, Eli Schein, Owner

Printed in the USA

TABLE OF CONTENTS

Contents

DEDICATION

Passed Away

Granny Shirley, GrandPop, Aunt Irlene, Aunt Josie, Pop Pop, Mars, Aunt Debbie, Granny Sara, Mom mom Fink's, Uncle Pratt, Massi, Fresh AKA T.J., Brandon AKA B, My old head Wally Gusto, Fat Butchie, Kev, Nert, Muhammad, Braheern, Fat Donald, Fat Billy-my brother from another mother, Black Mick, B-Black, Lil G, Booby, Buzz, Fat Malik, Trustee, Dawud, Lil Jawilly, Macywood, Whistle, Doug, Titty, Big Khalil, Juicy, DM AKA Pimp, Jameel, Lil Vel, Mom Parker, Basil, Kev, Lil Juicy, Daquan Ratcoon, Black Al, God Mom Ms. Peck, Essi, White Boy Don, Joesph, Daquan Crump, George Monk Smith, Joey Crack, Ron Carter. **To my family Jamil Abdul Haqq's Daughter Keisha and to my brother Talib Torain—never forgotten.**

ACKNOWLEDGMENTS

Alhamdvlillah—All praise be due to ALLAH for allowing me to achieve certain goals in my life.

Thanks to all those who supported me by purchasing "Hidden Agendas" A street classic.

Now I must thank **my mom** Carolyn who holds a special spot in my heart love you mom and **my sisters** Marg and Meeka who went all out to get Hidden Agendas to the people, Love y'all and **my wife** Hallimah who played her part when it counted the most. To my Uncle Shakur, my Uncle Malik, to my pop Talib Alim, **my sisters** Mimi, Khadijah, Deon, my Aunt Sharon, Aunt Evelyn, Aunt Milly, Aunt Jeanne.

MY COUSINS: Debbie, Pratt, Ronda, Big Hawky, Robert Speed, Niamah, Nikeya, Lil Kia, Milmil, Sha, Taheerah M, Ronny, Stella H, Tim T, Jasmonae, Anwar, Splendor, Serenity, Hamiyd, Sonya, Shirley, Tahira W, Amy, Shoni, Lajeana, Roro aka Choc, Emirea, Larry, Mookie, Joe the Boss, Stafakhan, Beez, Migel, Dew, Lexus, Mercedes, Lil Derrick, Boo Boo, Waleisha, Damon, Bert, Tanisha, Stacy, Beana, Brandon, Brianna Monae. **My nieces** Steph, Bree, Delly, Cece, Reema, Keeairah. **My nephews** Lil Lib Jr. **My heart,** Lyle, Zubayr, and Zady. Tyree, Tyhir, Tammy. **My daughters** Sobby, and Ranisha and **my beautiful Grandchild** Autumn.

Biglex, Taheerah, Feesah, Crystal, Judie, To my **56th and Master family** Khari, Nafis, Unc Blue, Azim, Lester, Dennis **keep your head up. Insha Allah you're on your way**. Toddy, J-Rock, Turtle, ChickenWing, Hilly, L-Gravy, Fat Mike, Dinky, Diddy, Lil Vinny, Bronco, Kidney Keith, L-Roy, Kasheem, Ronny James, Vern, Hassan in the Feds, Nell, Black Magic, Saboo, Yaya, Lov, Fat Ed, Cutty Raw, Yotti, E-money

Bag, Gate, Roosevelt **49th Street**, Wicked Wanda, Lazette, Nafeesa, Nichole, Lil kiya, Kita, Reese, Shanice, Aishah, Carla, Chante, Finks, Mumu, O-Dog and Black Delacy Street Bumpy Face Darnell, Laronda, Bubbles, Hisha, Regina, Ant Live **17th and Jefferson, To all the Smalls Family** Taheerah B, Leah, Sheshe, Shelly, Lisa, Linda, Monica, and Joyce. Amira Bud, Rafic aka Slim **Stay strong homey**, Gene Bird **my brother major love**, Shake **62nd and Felton thanks homey for showing love when it counted**. Michelle Parker, Rat-Rat, Emily, Roberta, DeDe, **all the Parkers Ya'all showed love on my 1st Novel**. Lasheeka, Tiffany Harris, Shirley Philips, Joseline, Sunny Carolina Va, Ms. Shirley, Amina, Bernard, Kiya, Big Merrel, Old Head Haneef, Danielle, Yolanda, Mahasin, **TEZ Caught In The Life is coming soon**, to my brother Mikell Davis **Stepping Stone Publishing**, Big Girly, Cisa Sanchez, Kev Sanchez, Anwar Shanchez, Boony, Kiya, Yana, Big Maze, Old head Hop up Dallaz, Abdul Haqq, lil Rock, Old head Naim, Black Tiffany from Chester, to my man "RO" **bringing you "Closed Mouth"** A Classic, Steph, SouthWest Ali the president of G.S ENT His wife Kinisha, His niece Stephanie, SouthWest ANH and Horizon Book Store, Xanyell Smalls, Nasir, Sheed the Bottom, Lils, Jeff, Poo AKA Laown, Thatcher AKA Will, Free, Ste-Al, Ty my brother love you homey, Cliff Vine Street, Jay Mississippi, Yaya, RootReds, Trini, Fareed AKA Larry, Muyty, George Santiago, AKA Uncle G, Pone, Skeen, Mase From North, Black, Ashlei F. Guy, Thanks to the person that purchased the first copy of "Hidden Agendas" a classic Carl Smith. Kareemas Book Store on 22nd and Jackson south philly, Black's and Noble Hakim, Meermeer, South Philly Neg and Teefy, Ashley.

SYNOPSIS

This book takes you on a journey inside the mind of a hustler where you get to witness how deep his vision is. Enclosed is Sixty Hot Titles that the streets and even common folk can relate to that will no doubt touch home.

Stop Hating

I aint maino but Hi haters, got the same question why haters, yaw wanksters turn waiters, I ride wit my crew yaw traitors, never stepping out my circle, cause I'll hurt you, break your heart, like Lauren did Steve Erkal, smoked alot of weed; but I prefer purple, I'm the reason you made bail, no price tag, but the chicks for sale, so stop acting like you up, you don't have no real bread so stop fronting, I'll come around deer season, and start hunting, still the same size cause I'm munching, get head from your girl on the low, cause you lunching, you aint gotta ask around, when Gotti touching, never stand in line I'm busting, one false move and I'll murk you, thought you got out on my boys, but they jerked you, call me daddy now cause I birthed you, heard you smashed a piper, and she burnt you, it's 6:00 way pass your curfew, check my squad you know what Bert do.

K. Gotti

DNA

DNA proved to be the truth, sorry baby girl for missing your whole youth, prom and graduation but I'm here now so congratulations, I wish I could turn back the hands of time, but this aint back to the future, we gotta move on and plan for the future, plus the newborn, on top of that your my first born, and that means alot, so call me daddy and pop pop, even though I won't be there when the baby drops, but I can still send gifts, and my family can flood the little one with a kiss; In my absence, I'm trying come home soon no plans on maxing, chilling with my grand kid relaxing, no matter the trials and tribulations I never denied you, even though I feel like I deprived you, whatever your career goals are I'm right behind you, and you can never do wrong in my eyes, I will tell you the truth, that'll over shadow the lies, not pointing the finger, that aint my agenda; I see you was born in the nineties, took you along time to find me, can't imagine what you been through, but I'ma step up and make it do what it do, your going to be eighteen so I can't give you a curfew, but I'ma protect you with my last breath, only cause I birthed you.

K. Gotti

Formidable Opponent

Have a heart, for what I never finish what I start, put the guns down, no all they respect is the spark, workout dog stay sharp, I move the weight like a shark, action speaks louder then words, I push those birds, you can't fly, not at all, I'm trying move a million eight balls, stay in that lane, all I know is the game, its time for a change, I'll think about it after I cop the Range, that's insane, I do it for the fame, That can cause alot of things to pop off, I'll blow a cats top off, I can't do life, I'll hold down 'my kids and my wife, just aint right, I don't think twice, what about your health, to busy trying count my wealth, very bad asthma, I'm playing video games on a 72" plasma, your crazy, gotta support the babies, get a 9 to 5 job, to late I'm married to the mob, the stakes are high, its do or die, its not worth your life, only if the price is right, that can be a very bad ending, I only finish the way I started in the beginning.

K. Gotti

Payback

Told you I was coming back, hold ya head relax, I'm pushing it to the max, your a good catch, no bait on the fishing rod, love your style and the way you ride, with no strings attached, it has to be the real cause you don't know how to act, your my gun in a holster I stay strapped, no matter what you always had my back, you remained on my mind when I was walking that track, trying gather my thoughts, I'm sticking to the script it's the way I was taught, ten in and still aint short, to much time to do it for sport, real love that can't be brought, my whole team trying get back in court, and beat the charges like Rocky, even with the hold against me they can't stop me, New York connect get it cheap from poppa, if I choose that route, moving books from the east to the south, new hustle, like Nipsy Russle, No cards but I still shuffle, money bags as weights to strengthen my muscles, I'm fed up, even when I'm down I hold my head up, I'll put it all on the line, before I give my man up, call me Teflon Don, the way I'm ducking these bullets, cats on the row, the haters hoping they pull it, the chamber like Duncan on green mile, I'm chasing Eminem running 8 miles, Gotti got it like Juvenile, cocky and I been confident, 9 years on the bench, like a enbanc, no hearing, dudes still dying and swearing, put they hand on the bible, I'm the neighbor hood idol, no superman, but I'm flying, like an eagle, I'm state property without Beanie Segal, no hate towards him, I just been doing time way before him, so give me props, got framed by dirty cops, no justice, just a rotten system, my dead brother I miss him, so his little kids I kiss'em.

K. Gotti

DRIVEN

Driven by the struggle, tired of seeing mom doing doubles clothes; food everything from the muscle 12 years old I had to hustle two sisters one brother, the opposite of Run & Russell, no Krush Groove, eyes on the prize watching the packs move, this is my life with nothing to lose, pride in the way with something to prove, be broke or get rich you choose I never had it easy, the block had my back cause the cats were so greasy 130 packs were my baby, no Lil Weesy, perfect picture but nobody sees me; so I keep pushing like precious! everything I got is a blessing, back and forth to jail, didn't learn my lesson No church so no confession, pay attention class is in session and I'm the teacher, real facts no preacher my family is my world so I'm treat ya, but aint no money worth your life; blood ties no price, married to yaw no rice and I aint walking down the aisle, I still think about yaw even living amongst the wild, so I try harder; trying to get the break like Nell Carter; I grew up alot smarter, blame it on the prison, I want the whole world to see my vision, and the way I brain storm, still children no corn, alot of lives torn, so I fault myself, only cause of the lack of wealth, pushing to put my book on the shelf, let that be the reason, hustle hard no matter the season, those who counted me out they only committed treason.

K. Gotti

SECRET CRUSH

Your my secret crush, what I gotta do to make it
all about us, the letter and cards should make
you understand, that I'm. really trying be your
man sky's the limit, I wouldn't do it if my heart
wasn't in it, tired of keeping my feelings hidden,
trapped in a closet, he don't really love you lets
be logic, your living fairy tales, don't talk on the
phone that much I learned that from Bronx Tale
It's like were on a small island, watchin' the boats
sail, I miss seeing you and sending you mail,
haven't heard from you in a while, hope your
doing swell, I'm attracted to your body features
plus your smell, your not the average chick can't
you tell, even though it's ten to one if I can't have
you then I don't want none dress in all black but
far from a nun. I aint trying put you under the
gun, I wanna take you on vacation and lay you
under the sun, message you from head to toe,
you mean alot to me I just want you to know,
don't leave cause I don't want you to go, no
bubbles but baby I'ma blow, give me one chance
to romance, I'm taking you out meeting people
at sundance, and that aint all, I'ma work hard so
we both ball, buy you that restaurant that you
always wanted, always play my part never fronted,
and if they ask who did it just say Gotti stunted,
to fulfill your dreams, lets do it as a team, and
walk the black carpet, we gotta fight for this like
Al Sharpton.

K. Gotti

Reality Check

Sister in the hospital body heavily sedated, out of surgery I'm just happy she made it, now the road to recovery, when I first heard the news it really was bugging me, like stress .on the brain, my cousin right down the hall his situation still aint changed, but there's still hope, true facts no joke, it's funny how we take life for granted, family in the background trying not to panic, stay strong I love yaw and I aint being romantic, real cat better yet a cannon, tubes down your throat so you can't talk, that's how the world should be so they can just walk the walk, I'm your brother so know I'm speaking from the heart, get well it's like getting a fresh start, and that's rare when coming out of the operational chair, but your not leaving this earth, until you receive your worth, everything that's written, I'm telling the truth I aint kidding, you gotta take care of yourself when your winning, and that doesn't mean money, your more important than that honey, do you and your children stop chasing dummies, Broke dudes no money, can't put food on the table, you got your own spot and car so your able, to provide on your own, let them know everywhere they lay their hat aint their home, treat'em like dogs feed'em bones, I hate Jody and Tyrone, I wish I could spit this to you on the phone. No Diddy or Dirty Money, but God willing I'm coming home.

K. Gotti

One Tear Later

How you sell your soul, instead of following your goals, now it's time to patch up the air holes, get your life back on track, put away the condoms and stop walking that track, the streets claim lives, the tricks tell lies, to get in your pants, your worth more then a pole dance, to many diseases and infections leaves one taking pills and painful injections, your worth more then that, and I don't gamble but I'm willing to bet, you don't gotta sell drugs, you deserve kisses and hugs and all the above, don't let society judge, why you around those thugs, they don't have your best interest, all they want is interest, off your body parts, to continue to live a lavish life style, no dad makes you a bastard child but fight back for your right's to be a lady, and help raise the crack babies, never give up, pull your panties up, stop showing your butt, mind frame is corrupt, do anything for a few bucks, your a queen not a duck, go back to school, now that's what's up, change your ways, look forward to better days, it doesn't get any worse, alot of pain, feeling like I'm cursed, no your confused by the haters, it's you baby one tear later.

K. Gotti

No Limit

I love my girl, she's my world, reminds me of a precious pearl, or a black diamond, this love is like stairs steady climbing, and it wouldn't work without two people behind it, go green change the climate, all I think about is trying climax, so my mind frame is fresh, real eager to change my address, relocate hoping the courts bite the bait, like a fishing rod, its been a long ride, I'm in over drive pushing a F150, just happy your here with me, don't celebrate Halloween so don't try to trick me, it didn't take you that much to get me, a 5-foot cutie, I respect your friends Lex, Fe, Tah, and Judy, and I'm loving your booty, facts of life no tootie, trying get money longer then Rudy's, or Bill Cosby, I'm hot and rap aint even my hobby, all I know is what turned out Whitney & Bobby, the streets robbed me, at a young age, never been shot so not a victim of the 12 gauge, 9 years trapped behind a cage will bring about the rage, but I remain humble cause it's light at the end of the tunnel, my team in a huddle, it's the industry we trying muscle, with blunt force, Gucci sneaks now, no more air force, working on my passport, so I can travel worldwide, when you broke it's a landslide, uneven, so I see why Sigel came with the reason, then the solution, take care your girls so they won't result to prostitution, that's rapid, the youth done started macking, without goldy, young girl turned on by the Rolly, it's

only a watch, got'em giving up the twat, just to
be down, until her body's found, in a vacant
lot by the cops, raped and gagged, fully aware
of the undercover fags, men dressed in drag,
boy is that sad.

K. Gotti

Love Jones

Me loving you is a understatement, its like we both destined for greatness, the bond is tight so how can they hate this, no Lox but we going make it, you got me in a maze, and I can't escape it, baby sorta like the matrix's, so I wouldn't be wrong .if I chased it, give me a test watch me ace it, and I didn't study, we lovers and buddies, so tell a friend, and your next of kin, cause I'm loving you to the end, so let the matrimony begin, no need to prolong, you with me is where you belong, no matter how long I'm going, you gotta stay strong, like Loretta Kings in your blood, I'm missing your kisses and your hug's, but its all love, I fall back ducking the lames & the plugs, to avoid getting caught up, being stupid aint the way I was brought up, to keep me from trying to touch down, that's like Shaq going for a touchdown, no more blunts they smoke Dutch now, I'm burning the clutch now, on a stick shift still in the field but aint trying pitch, millions on my mind call me Richy Rich or Crown Royal, its in me to get it until my body is rubbed down in oil, wrapped in a white sheet facing the east, right now I'm still in the jungle no beast, and the only time you get to eat is at the feast, can't complain cause its a treat, and a blessing from-above, in me is half passion half thug, but I do care, trying be there in a few months or the new year, new boots new gear, as long as I'm out of here.

K. Gotti

WHAT IF

What if steady B was on death row, and cool had life and a few numbers, and Aids didn't exist, it wouldn't be no need for rubbers, what if left eye aint die that night, and those 9/11 people aint take that flight, what if my man Billy aint die from those syrup & pills, and LC never lost her best friend from the hills, what if the dipset didn't break up, and Chris Brown and Rihanna never made up. What if Star Jones never got kicked off The View, and desert storm had no clue, what if Rodney King never got beat by the cops, and the hood wasn't really feeling the Lox, what if Lib, Nert and G were still alive, and Jennifer Hudson never signed with Jive, what if they sent all of us back to Africa, and there never was a lex st. massacre, what if Tyson aint do that rape, and Dame didn't get killed trying get that cake, what if Barack never won the election, and they gave Aron Jones the ejection, what if I never caught that case, and Jeff Gordon never won that race.

K. Gotti

Hi Haters

You dudes are runners, how a dude in jail got you changing your girls number; I'm wide awake while you cats are on the streets deep in slumber, 11 years down still got potential to do Bugati numbers, its double R's now, I let you lames drive the hummers, cause yaw running late like 11 summers, you remind me of dumb & dumber, I moved up in the world call me Mr. Drummer, and you reading my mail, that's hate on a major scale, picture you dudes keeping Gotti from trying prevail, that's like Steve taking over for Dave Chapelle, you got the same address I'm out the ATL, Living lavish, I'm the reason your chick is flooded with carrots, she got tired of living average, trips to Paris, you can take her hand in marriage, I'ma beast but call me a savage, and I hear you're insecure, you wouldn't be if she was secure. That's what happens when your not use to macking, I get money and I aint just rapping, so let my name taste like shit in your mouth, before I get like left eye and burn down your house, I'ma big dog with no time to play cat & mouse, I'm the east to what Scarface is to the south, I turn giants to Bow wow, and make'em roll bounce, so stop hating, I aint selling records but you boosting my ratings, and to you I'm considered a threat, can't help that I'm season vet.

K. Gotti

FAMILY TIES

Blood line is thicker then water, I'ma show love to your son's and your daughter, we just spoke on the phone, But I guess life is shorter, you told me you would figure it out. It's like you didn't have a choice. In my head I'm still hearing your voice, come on home I got you, it's going be tough living in this world without you, and we all gotta go just some before others, even though we was cousins, everybody thought we was brothers, same DNA different Mothers. How we let the game become us, that's something I'll never understand, I lost family members, friend's and my man, still I remained loyal never took the stand, I gave the hood everything even my left and my right hand. But got nothing back in return. No tears but my eyes still burn, all our lives we made the wrong turn. Now we gotta look pass all the lies, just so we can keep the family ties.

K. Gotti

Chasing Waterfalls

Stop chasing waterfalls. Baby your connected to a Boss, Always play for the win never except the loss, you can't recognize the real from the frauds, you don't have to step up to the plate, my stomach is full I already ate , I'm trying to get you your break, the next level, Foreign car's foot to the pedal, Show you how to live outside the ghetto, I'ma win the race without the gold medal, you could have it all if you didn't settle, Do it big, grow up and stop being a toys-R-us kid, and stop holding grudges, my beef ain't with you it's with the judges, Live dude you gotta love it, although some hate, I just wanna celebrate cause I made it; To the top, Part 2 Hidden Agendas til the casket drops.

K. Gotti

Counted Out

Damn D what happen to the help, you promised me, no matter how much money you got, you'll never be live as me, I remember when you had nothing, from the stand to the store, now you fronten, even called you a few times, no answer so I know you was ducking, how could you forget, same dude from the J who's known for hustling, you and Beez said yaw was going to the table, what about the first of the month when they cut off my cable, that can never be forgotten, all these years I knew you dudes were rotten, I just played my position, young bul with a deep vision, with hopes of never getting caught slipping, down 11 years with no desire to start snitching, this is hell without chefs kitchen. A few more people left me for dead; that I dare not mention, some days I feel like poison ivy, just minus the itching, the way I was venting, you would've thought I was bitching, but that's not the case, I'm only exposing a few fakes, and by dealing with them, I realized my mistakes, I never brought the temperature down, I raised the stakes, Bulletproof love for Gene Bird and Shake, I got yaw just waiting for a break, so I can share my plate.

K. Gotti

I GOTTA MAKE IT

I don't run track, so don't chase me, I'm just trying get rich, like the two chicks who started pastry, I was the star in my class, so the teacher aced me, I see the hate, that's why the lames wanted replace me, I'm behind the wall like a cat safe be, no combination, I Rep the Deen of Al-Islam without the nation, not out yet but the time still racing, Real dude's I'm embracing, can't sing, so I doubt if you'll ever catch me changing face's, Prada sneaks no laces, front row at the horse races, I'm chasing a fortune, look at all these women out here having abortions, I changed my lifestyle from drugs and extortion, Uncle Sam got his hand out telling me he want a portion, relationships falling apart everybody divorcing, crooked cops on the streets nobody's enforcing, I ain't trying make the Forbes list, I just wanna be rich, and buy us a fortress. Just gotta get past the misfortune, and setbacks, no list but they can check this, until it's even, alot of people are scheming, can't nobody knock you for dreaming, I don't care about those folks who's leaving, I got a chance as long as I'm breathing, Gotta get me a big plate, they raised the stake so much hate, and disloyalty in the hood, I don't have alot of friends so I'm good.

K. Gotti

Deeper Than Rap

So today is your birthday, it's like celebrating your birth place, more like Shirkday, or 29 years of sins, I seek refuge from shaytaan and the Jinns, contemplating on getting my soul cleansed. I'm dangerous with the pencil & pens, call it the gift & the curse, it's a meaning behind every verse, more powerful then a preacher at church, I know I commit sins no shirk, that's something that aint forgiving, so know that it's forbidden, it's three aspects and one's hidden, so you'll never know when your committing, such a violent act, can't take that back, unless you repent using taubah, I aint going hold ya, that's like a pot boiling over, the nights are hot and the days are colder, can't wait to put the jail on my shoulder, and secure my fam, I'ma do it without a stimulus plan, we going ball like Elton brand, no doubt we going to pay Uncle Sam, by filing taxes, I just want my days with you relaxing, on a California king, this is my dream, so don't wake me, if I do something wrong don't hate me, I be damn if I'ma let this jail stuff break me, on the street I be at the Masjid, the opposite of where mase be, getting all five until the day I die, baby don't cry, death is apart of life, just bury me Muslim since you'll be my wife.

K. Gotti

MISUNDERSTOOD

What you know about the struggle, daddy wasn't around mom she had to hustle, did everything from the muscle, wanted you to go to school and get the knowledge, had to prostitute just to get you thru college, not the lifestyle she envisioned, what could she do it was written, as a child her dreams were more vivid, son caught up in the streets, don't know if he's Blooding or Crippen, four women to himself now he's pimpin, any thing to survive, to stop the hunger pains and the lies, all mom can say is she tried, and people ask why. But they don't know about the nights she cried, sitting in her room Dumbhigh, that's life in the ghetto. It's deeper than heavy metal, so blame it on the environment. The children are her circle, so respect her conglomerate, no money at the round table black n white TV no cable, rats and mice are taking over feeling like life is over, contemplating suicide, cause in the hood it's black on black genocide with poverty still on the rise, the recession made it even harder, her oldest son doing life, hoping Barack gives him a pardon her daughter follows in her footsteps, selling sex to accumulate a check.

Nothing but headaches and built up stress,
praying that the pain is put to rest, Doesn't
know her next move, like a game of chess,
Thinking that it can't be this hard, it has to be
a test, still living so she's blessed with the crack
and dope, there's no hope, and the future
looks smaller than a scope, don't you get it my
lifestyle is wicked, I'm addicted.

K. Gotti

No Matter The Distance

Now listen, no matter how far the distance, us being together it has to be written, so me trading you in, you gotta be kidding, me having you is better then winning, so I'ma do whatever to keep you grinning, my love for you can never be hidden, I'm a real dude, I thought you knew that from the beginning, the love I got is never ending, I gotta speak my mind. I can't do no pretending, so peep the verse, I'ma feel this way until I'm placed in a hearse, It's like a gift & a curse, cause love hurts, but I can stand the pain, cut from a different cloth, so that might seem strange, your the only woman I'm trying to claim, all I want is you, with nothing else to gain, money, I get my own change, born bread winner, the opposite of the lames, pass the stress more like sex on the brain, all angels, your cookies I'm trying to mangle, from· the inside out, now that's what I'm talking about, I'ma always be me, even without the clout, and you aint gotta worry about, another chick mentioning my name, they want king of pressure plus the fame, but I'm out the game, so my lifestyle changed, I'ma still wear that shit, it's been that way since I was six, but don't trip, you'll still look good in the Hijab plus the Prada & Gucci kicks, you my wife so you'll always be the shit, so excuse my French.

K. Gotti

SO DIFFICULT

Can't wait to have you in the shower, rather for ten minutes or an hour, our lovemaking is like money & power, the opposite of other folks, better yet different strokes, without Arnold & Will, baby you fit the bill, trying exceed the limit on sex skills, give you the raw deal, uncut sort of like Nip Tuck, sucking your clit and licking the coochie lips, I'm tryin to OD off your shit, all night long, you're on my mind like an R&B song from trey Songz, can't help but wait to catch my first break, and get me a taste, of that good n plenty, so much sperm backed up in me, the wet dreams be explosive, like a bomb, trying to reap the benefits from my crime, so tired of doing time, it's a lesson learned, no bridges did I burn, I'm married to the firm, still being patient waiting my turn, your love is what I yearn, like never before, I'm shooting to the core, white sand off shore, baby you I adore, who could ask for more, having you is like going on tour, cross country, or city to city, can't be mad for having someone so pretty.

K. Gotti

Reminisce

Your more then just a good catch, I think you got the best sex, it's in my mind cause I aint have it yet, I still Reminisce on the day we met, your whole demeanor had me flexed, that's why I overdosed on compliments cause you looked good, and was feeling a live cat from the hood, Like I knew you would, I came with new flavor, just wanna be closer then neighbor's, I studied you that whole night like you was my major, never been to college, I'm just being logic, your beauty is hypnotic, and we our a good match, like Jada and Will, I'll take you over the mills, I'm just keeping it real, your love is worth more then a dollar bill, just need out so I can exercise my skills, and pick up the tab of paying the bills as I should, trust me if I was out I would, lift the burden, for certain. Late night's me and you closing the curtains, Having sexy fun I'm just trying to cum, and lick you from head to toe, I'm just in love with you baby, don't mean to be Joe, welcome to the the loving you show, it's sold out, cause I want you all alone, I'm just trying to make it home, before Tyrone try to take my place, even though I'm still in the race, Trying to beat this case, I'm passed first base, aiming for a home run, like Derek Jeter success never taste sweeter, time is running out like a car meter, so I'll never let the game come between us.

K. Gotti

In My Own Lane

I'm glad you loving the bars, I'm trying start our own football team, like Nelly, on the longest yard, there's no McNabb, it's you baby I'm tryin snatch and grab, I'm gang related minus the do rag, the bread is the only thing that makes my pants sag, so now I carry credit cards, Black and Platinum so that's what's happening, without, Roger and Big Shirley, never late always early, and never rerunning stay gunning for the win, my whole life be surrounded around sin, streets never taught me morals, only how to hustle and get oral, no doubt honor amongst thieves, addicted to that paper the same color as leaves, I just picture me making cats bleed, nothing violent, to much talent, to get caught slipping, it's not the game I'm missing, it's you and my kin folk, that's real no joke, not Eddie Griffen but I'm going for broke, put it all on the line, like a burning house going up in smoke, no life insurance, so my blood's pouring, like hell razor, at the end of the day who's going save ya, not mom cause she made ya, It's not possible, in life it's always obstacles, to cross, in my household I'm Charles in charge, not giving up until I get that discharge, that's the whole plan, murdered the game like son of Sam, my squad like the black Klu Klux Klan, not racist, chasing the big faces.

K. Gotti

ADDICTED

Call you heroin, cause baby I'm addicted, a line drawn like your love is restricted, who could've predicted, that we would take it this far, marriage, big house, fancy cars, living like stars, without Hollywood, we rich but still keeping it hood, I aint the clipse but I'm good, as long as I got you, if this was teenage love I'll break my curfew, cause I wouldn't let nothing keep us apart, its more than my love its my heart, when it comes to you I'm a shark, without the water, let me place my order, let your dad know I'm in love with his daughter, give 'em props cause he taught her, how to be a lady, I'm real protective over my baby, I like Eminem but I aint shady, Just in love with a girl who was born 11/5/80, she drives me crazy, everything she does never seems to-amaze me, you're a diamond in the rough, this love is tough but it's us, loyalty, honor & trust, we deserve that much, never falling off even in the clutch, gotta switch gears, this our year, trying outshine our peers, mind racing like spiral stairs, the relationship is rare, but I'm all for it, I seen it without Dione Warrick, if its a crime I can't report it, a bus ride I'ma board it, to reach my destination, giving you my all on no hesitation, sex, love, mad penetration, this aint the basics, I'm on your ass like a fresh pair of asics, I'm making a statement, real cat face it, aint no replacing me, play the DVD, watch me live in living color there's no other ask my mother, I made you my other half, since I lost my brother.

K. Gotti

BITTERSWEET

Call you the mail lady, the way the letters flow, everyday I tell myself I gotta go, just to make it even, won't be content until my whole family's deening, that shahadah statement has a heavy meaning, gotta be married before I can fill you with semen, or we both will be in the hereafter grieving, for illegal sex, it's not a game of chess, a real life episode, and a day of Bold & Beautiful, baby this love is musical, no sound, I just love having you around,it makes me happy, me without you, is like a dude trying slap me, a fresh bid no rappy, imagine someone trying clap me, I'm not alone, I got you in back of me, so I feel better, a black soft leather, us falling back enjoying the weather, trying win like Floyd Mayweather, a few losses, on top of a few crosses, but I'm focused, eyes on the prize, History filled with lies, I take the bitter with the sweet and ride, with no brakes, all I need is one break, to make thing's happen, on point now, no· longer slacking in this jail, they steady racking, up on bodies, I'm trying step out with you beside me, jailing done got boring. I should be on the streets scoring, and deep in that kitty cat hearing it roaring, why the lames still broke warring.

K. Gotti

It Ain't Over

All the compliments in the card, had me in a foreign land Russian, and no doubt a discharge is the top of discussion, on top of a little mercy, I could eat you like a chocolate Hershey, yes the courts jerked me, outside the guidelines, to give me a whole lot of time, but I'm still fighting, like Mike Tyson biting, and the grip is held tight, a little relief will be just right, but I'm patient, pay back is in the making, like the movie precious, just having you is a blessing, can't wait to get that private session, like a strip club, no pole, just my lips in your hole, heart beating as you moan, and you are number one, So don't never question that, I got rid of those chicks from way back, And if they come I do know, Cause you told me so, all I want is you no other place to go, My love is real no show, and I ain't never been good with acting, so don't be insecure, you and my family are the ones I'm trying secure, with my last breath, it's us to the death, and I know you need me like a heartbeat, that's one of the reason to keep me out the streets, do everything I can to make sure we eat, all Halaal, even eat at Bilal's garden your love is my target, never shopping at the house of Bargain, no longer on the corner trying meet the margin, I'm the captain and the Sgt., so follow my lead, while I get that cheese, and put the Kinfolk at ease, one more chance please, cover my mouth when I sneeze, so I don't spread the Germ, I'm allergic to the worms.

K. Gotti

TRUE STORY

All I know is the game, Lord knows I wanna change, I'll do anything to stop the hunger pain's, never been obsessed with the fame, nothing to lose a whole lot to gain, all I got is three hots and a cot, and Salaat, mom was always around, where was pops, when the pain going stop, late nights hugging the block, nightmares running from the cops, chasing fiends with million dollar dreams, this is my life, far from a scheme, I did it all without a team, on the inside the grass ain't always green, so how would you know if I was starving, I sold crack for living, never sung a song like Marvin, so excuse me darling, if you don't understand, I was a boy who became a man, the street's raised me, and the jails aged me, from 18 to 32, so what am I supposed to do, pray the police get booked so I can sue, my situation is desert storm, without a clue. If you only knew, what I been through, drug addiction's, that led to an overdose, ain't no champagne to raise a toast, only thing left is hope, that I make it, never been known to fake it, time served I'ma take it, this cycle gotta break it, cause I don't wanna come back again, I started the movie, now this the end.

K. Gotti

PERFECT PICTURE

Baby every time I go to sleep I dream about you and when were apart all I'm doing is thinking of you. The sight of your face sends chills down my spine, never thought I would have to work this hard to make you mine; you're sexy from head to toe. I pray this night never has to go. Lights camera action making love to you is my satisfaction when you cry. I'll lick the tear drops from your eyes the day we got together was my reward better yet my prize always telling you the truth never having to worry about the lies. Caring for you is my burning desire our love for each other will overcome any trial and tribulations that lovers face inside this cold world. You touch my soul in a way you couldn't imagine this love is like pure magic without tricks I find it hard to get past our first kiss the things I have plan for us is written on a long list like a Kodak moment so baby picture this.

K. Gotti

UNBREAKABLE

It's a blessing to be tied in marriage, success baby so we won't live average, I love you minus the carrots, your pretty as a colorful parrot, nights out together horse and carriage, trips to Paris, you're more than my wife your my heart, I'm the red circle on the board you're the dart, you're the full package plus the spark, it's like your the whale and I'm the shark, swimming in a big tank, life jackets so we won't sink, I'm the pen and you're the ink, until it's dried up, no magazine but this word up, our relationship started small, look how it's blown up, and I wouldn't change it for the world, only cause your one special girl, Ten diamonds Ten pearls top of the line jewels, it's you I choose, I've won so why would I wanna lose, your the pieces to my puzzle, and the reason I have no desire to hustle, except legal, I'm in the law library like a certified paralegal, Aiming for a win, love it when you smile excited when you grin, your closer then my next of kin, and I ain't breaking the family ties, that's like committing a sin, your love makes me tipsy, without the juice and gin, a long story to tell, where do I begin, I wanna help raise your boy's to men, lost a lot of people but your my best friend, Never break the bond, I'm in love with Ms. Bond, No joke, far from a hoax, It's deeper then a nose snorting coke.

K. Gotti

Feel My Pain

Some days I sit ln my bed and brainstorm, my body's cold, but my heart's warm, its like my life's torn, in two halves, gotta keep going, can't dwell on the past, I need you to stay strong, since you're my better half doing what I can to accumulate some cash, trying get other folks to tap in their stash, baby my life style is fast, I knew the drug game wouldn't last, so I switched my profession, still alive so that's a blessing, I know who's real now that's a lesson, Eager to get that private session, when the cuffs are off, now who's boss, Gotti or Rick Ross, middle finger to Geroff, still smiling even with the loss, who said freedom didn't cost, A pretty penny, survival is in me, like blood running through my veins, Just waiting patiently for my situation to change, I'm on their ass with a perfect aim, still got my eyes on that 2012 Range, I'll take the success over the fame, It's a perfect picture no frame, my whole life addicted to the game, my old friends ain't acting the same, I'm in my own lane, you're stuck on my brain, It'll break my heart to see you with those lame's, you gotta feel my pain.

K. Gotti

COLD WORLD

Money don't fold, so much Ice I'm catching a cold, so keep going to the gym doing crunches, I'm at the bank putting the hundreds in bunches, And I give'em out like free lunches, you marks can't touch us we munchin overweight like Rick Ross, what can I say? I'm a boss, Chinese chicks no sauce, stop sign so the CL600 on pause, summer time so I'm drawling, no job so I'm Balling, cut my phone off cause the connect keep calling, Like he can't smell the smoke, three bricks plus some liquid dope, he thought it was a Hoax, But nope, he's burnt like grill cheese, gotta smoke a blunt to keep me at ease, my broad in the background screaming please, don't do it, but it's too late I'm knee deep, so I gotta pursue it, the show ain't over it just started, the whole world can smell me like I farted, the flow' is retarded, and I'm as real as it gets, I get' em 10.5 brick, Black Porche I call it KIT, bought wifey the BENT, Money earned money spent, own houses so no rent, ain't Fonz Worth Bently, but I'm G and A Gent, and I'm make 'em pay, I got a few groupies who look like Charney from Ray Jay, and I ain't never been petty, take chicks out but we never go steady, So she better be ready, to get naked, cause time is hectic, and even though I'm not signed with Grand Hustle, I'm still doin' shit from the muscle, mind state like Russell, yaw od'eing off mad dog, I'm trying to come up like Madoff.

K. Gotti

Bonnie And Clyde

All I got is my word, I doubt if I'ma break it, in the back of my mind, It's like are we really going make it, the break I need I know I gotta take it, I'm just being real I can't fake it, and your kids are your priority, sometimes I feel alone, like I'm the minority, no success stories. Just the struggles, How a broke nigga going to cuddle, it's like I was born to hustle, and my goals are so far apart, no lights in the house I'm sleeping in the dark, no tears I'm speaking from the heart, my hands are tied, But I still ride, with no choice, don't you hear the pain in my voice! A whole lot of turmoil: either a 9 to 5 or cook it to the oils, call me dirt created from the soil, so go ahead and revamp, I'm trying relamp, see some day light, this is my life, and your problems are mine, since you'll be my wife, don't fall apart, stay sharper then a knife, can't let your baby daddy see you sweat, this is all part of the test, So we aim for the win until we are put to rest, modern day Bonnie and Clyde we the best, from the east coast to the west, stop worrying about Burning miles, Baby we above the clouds.

K. Gotti

CAN'T WAIT FOR THAT DAY

Like a kid with no job, looking for tax returns, in jail you do extra sets to get that burn, have no choice but to stand firm, no doubt you're my other half, take you shopping let you throw it in the bag, don't look at the price tags, picture me running drag, I leave that to the fakes and the fags, anything you did wrong I put that in the past, can't you tell? That's how much I'm loving your ass, your a star the other chicks are trash, I'm stuck to you like a baby catching a diaper rash, these doors open up we can have our own bash, party like when Frank was home, I'm just eager to get you all alone, give it to you raw no shot of patron, Baby I'm in the zone, like my minds blown, so live I need to be cloned, I speak the real, while others act like dogs choking on bones, cheer up cause daddy's home; it's been along time coming, do anything to keep you cumming, put it in hard drive, I'm tucking my pride, so just enjoy the ride, that Dorney Park couldn't provide, all I see is us on the rise, like Barack and Michelle, two people trapped in a shell, This love is a spell, drink you like a bottle of Ginger ale, no acid, our relationship is a moderate day classic, so the hate we gotta look past it, Trips to the park with the picnic basket, let the kids play, can't wait for that day.

K. Gotti

This Is My Life

Look how the game changed, one minute you balling, next minute you falling, And you can't get up, 20 to 40 it's like you ran out of luck mind racing like what the fuck, this is how it's going end, lost two of my closest kin, in my cell all alone no friend, this is my life of sin, can't blame it on the juice and gin, long story where do I begin, to much time to take it on the chin, the outcome when boy's become men, we ride the wrong route, Just to get that clout, From pack's to Brick's, and moving with the wrong click, No loyalty or trust, trapped in a drug bust, all they know is God we trust, that green paper, look how the game rape ya; either dead or in jail, no lawyer sitting on a million dollar bail, all for the gun's and scale's price tag like my life's for sale, Part 1 of living in hell, Dead bodies adapted to the smell, small turtle no shell, face exposed, hit with hard blows, do in court hoping no one shows, so much pain from my head to my toes, this is my life nobody knows, that's why they judge me, Even though I put the world above me, through the gates my mom hug me, only cause she love me, the game ain't pretty it's ugly, No proactive, can't go forward so I pedal backwards, this is my life no actress, or a movie script, either you broke or rich, the streets was my nitch, no bat so I pitch.

K. Gotti

TEARS OF A HUSTLER

Every teardrop Represents the struggle, Mind racing like Bill Gates so I still hustle, trying make it out the ghetto like Russle, without Krush groove, the game is bisexual either you win or lose, Free will so you gotta choose, Block the greed from my heart, to x out the spark, I see the light although the path is still dark, I'ma small fish surrounded by sharks, with lock jaws, My life was a speed dial until jail put it on pause, Not Chinese but I duck frauds, Half man Half dog, so beware, I bite harder then Health Care, I'm the real I don't have to swear, Pretty woman like Richard Gere, but they lack loyalty, what can I say my mom spoiled me, At a young age, keep reading turn the page, the story is Heart felt, No ring but still holding the belt, For being a stand up dude my fault didn't mean to be rude, cause I don't know about snitching, I scratch my own back when it starts itching, And I hold water even in the trenches, but still I was left for dead, by a few comrades and a few old heads, I use a sheet to tuck 'em in after I put 'em to bed, because Betrayal is worse then death, It's Bulletproof love for Real cats tatted on my chest, No ink cause that's a curse; If I was you I would put this verse back in reverse, so you could better comprehend, I ain't going back even if the connect got it for ten, All legit now no more indulgin' in sin, A million ventures I'm determined to win, I spent my whole life inside the sijin.

K. Gotti

FEELING MYSELF

Rather I win or lose, I'm still stand tall like Rocky, chick's thought I was coke, the way they tried to cop me, but I'm married with children, my worth way up in the millions, light skin green eyes they think I'm Sicilian, not grinding on the block no more, but I'm still making a killing like Charles Manson, no condo, six bedroom mansion, Black may-back, this is payback, from way back, for you cats who shitted on me, Chinchilla minks the tailors put it on me, designer shoes, 7 day cruise, catching me is like Mission Impossible without Tom Cruise, I been in slumps like Martin with nothing to lose, I'm the modern day hill street blues, yaw hustling backwards yaw fools, get up get out following the rules, don't get caught slipping cause with the Fed's there's no more pimping, or bottle popping, unless you fold over, your rat now game over, I'm still me, with the jail on my shoulder's, wifey right behind me in that Red Range Rover, she deserves it for making every court appearance, the wealth is apparent, why hide it, can't die wit it, so I divide it, amongst my team, so we all live the American dream, came along way from serving those fiends, spend so much it's like Ben Franklin is my genes, never cover my face when I sneeze, spraying all you haters, and I protect my family, like Buffy the vampire slayer.

K. Gotti

Daddy's Little Girl

Sobby your daddy's little girl, even though I'm not there, you're still my world, not a diamond, more like a pearl, but your love is priceless, and your getting older, So I know I gotta mold ya, kiss you and hold ya, never scold ya, teach you what's right and what's wrong, dress you in HiJab no thong, more then determined, I'm prone, miss seeing you on visits, and talking to you on the phone, it's like your whole life I been gone, like history repeating itself, and that same old song, but I promise you I'm different from my pop, I would never leave you behind like leftover stock, Before you was born I had trouble with the cops, which caused my incarceration, you being my daughter is a celebration, like a 12th grade graduation, even though I didn't finish school, too busy breaking all the rules, young but far from a fool, I used the streets as a tool, just to make ends meet, having you as my daughter is a treat, and I'm fighting to the end, with no sign of defeat, wasn't trying to starve, so I had to eat, It's just your dad talking, and keeping it street. I'm down right now, But I'll be to get you, when I reach my peak.

K. Gotti

Betrayal

I must've been crazy making you my other half, when my brother passed, you ain't my BM but you still trash, I kept it real without the dick suck and the ass, never graduated but still ahead of my class, you make me sick like a rash on a baby's ass, plus swine flu, your confused no clue, In my mind I'm like what did I do, nothing just an excuse to justify you frontin, you chose a lame over a cat that's munching, I don't talk smack in each verse I'm saying something, left the streets alone but I'm still hustling, Raping the industry, I trusted you more then those who were kin to me, but that's all over, so thank me later, I put you in the circle with all the haters, it's Gotti and Kareem how could you betray us, everything built off lies, I lost my appeal but damn if I ain't try, the clock is still ticking, what can I say it was written, you crossed me and that forbidden, to caught up to know the real you was hidden, Jim Carey Black Mask, I gave you the game so you could get some cash, Book company Publishing, to stop your stomach from rumblin', and this how you pay me back, I'm back to pimping just minus the track, chick's all flavors, I knew I made it when I had Will Smith as my neighbor; I'm just joking around trader, 2011 Escalades, no Rap rader, I told you It'll get greater later, Just had no patience, you act like you was the only one waiting.

K. Gotti

All Or Nothing

If I could do it all again, I promise to do it different, why the whole philly had to start snitching, I hold my water even in the trenches, another chance is the only thing I'm wishing, I'll give you everything without your permission, fall back relax let me do the dishes, all I want you to do is flood me with kisses, while we both sit down and count our riches, success I'm addicted, how could you blame me, my whole life I been poverty stricken, came a long way from pitching, you and a few others are the only ones I'm missing, that's why I'm on a mission, to get that win, and get released from the pen, A new start we begin, marriage with children, it's such a beautiful feeling, so I'm reaching for the ceiling, pass the obstacles, to get to the millions, that green paper with the eagles, own casino's like Bugsy Segal, mind state illegal, with good intentions, the whole world is my witness, I mean business, everything in the open, nothing hidden, so lames stop pretending.

K. Gotti

Ace Of Spade

Like Michael Basien men cry in the dark! I just want a shot at the title, so I can play my part, the streets taught me how to cook, without culinary arts, just trying stay above sea level, when swimming with the sharks, I'm a human dart, aiming for the heart, and I'm innocent, but they still wanted fry me, like Tookie, I turned down the deal, and took the Judge to trial, found guilty, mind frame still focused on getting filthy, I only talk it cause I live it, I appreciate the game like an up state visit, I want all the bread, rather mills or small digits, keep a bad chick 6 feet or a midget, talking marriage, she must be exquisite, never hustled where I shitted, still balling so I pivot, nothing left to gain, cause I did it, get rich or die trying, let me take that back cause I'm lying, aint no money worth dying, if the hood flooded, you know who's supplying, you had your turn so stop crying, I aint the best, I'm great, no VHl, so no debate, counting me out was a mistake, I can't be replaced; like a deck of cards, I'm the only black of spade.

K. Gotti

No Father Figure

No father around, so I use to play craps in the play ground, trying make ends meet, young age addicted to the streets, all I wanted was new clothes new sneaks, and to be able to show love to my peeps, broken household, so the crack I sold, no change, only the money that fold, dropped out of ninth grade, Joined the school of hard knocks, 12 years old hugging the block, 13 caught my first case, mom had to pick me up at 8th and Race, family court in front of Judge Reynolds, cruising the neighborhood's in rentals, didn't have a dream, only drugs and fenes, got caught up, no dad just the way I was brought up, me and my brother had to share each others stuff, times was ruff, but we made it through, a five man crew, survival nothing to do, hand on the trigger, I blame you dad no father figure.

K. Gotti

Rich Habits

Have a baby by me girl, and be a millionaire, eight bedroom house platinum chandeliers, vacation spots with time shares, late nights on the beach we share, no fast chick, I like 'em square, college educated, just happy that we made it, this far, 5 star restaurants, foreign cars, black card no limit, so keep on spending, this is the life style you live when you winning, its like magic, in my blood is rich habits, most chicks are gold diggers & magnets, but have a baby by me and be buried in lavish, minks, diamonds, nothing average, Gucci & Prada baggage, she's addicted to the fashion, holes in the condoms so the sperm splashing, plus the tongue, no safety on the gun, shots everywhere, like the lights in times square, Carol's daughter success never smelt so sweet, my family smiles now when I flood 'em with gifts, they loving the treats, left the game alone no longer running the streets, I'm out in a foreign land where Spanish is their speech, what I got is well deserved for all the nights I couldn't eat, California King so at night I can sleep, some days it feels like my body's getting weak.

K. Gotti

BULLETPROOF

Don't need no ink, to tattoo your love on my chest, your not in the running, you won the race, like saving grace, so why settle for less, don't play football but your a good catch, the opposite of all the rest, I wear your love like a bulletproof vest, so ready to sign on the x, to secure this marriage, buried the old habits, now that were stuck like magnets, this is real big, nothing average, without the horse & carriage, this will be my first marriage, so I'm treating it special, drink H20 out the vessel, As a celebration, until I can get in those yams, and apply heavy penetration, No masturbation, cause that's a sin, weak at times, that's the Jinn in men, I ask myself how did we begin, Lovemaking won't be mixed in sin, call me Barack and you Michelle we'll be together, until we both prevail, won't stop trying to win even if we fail, that's the ups and downs of life, who cares as long as you're my wife.

K. Gotti

BEDROOM SECRETS

My love for you has grown stronger, I can feel it in my stomach its like a hunger, I want you bad how much longer, I'm patient, we been together for so long our love is ancient, but with classic tunes, can't wait to get you in the boom boom room, lick you from head to toe, don't mean to be Joe, don't blame me, I just want you to lay me, All night long, let me rip off your thong, straight to those lips with a wet kiss, its you I miss, while I work hard to get rich, but remain humble, lay in the bed and watch that pretty soft ass tumble, your pussy is in my mouth that's why I mumble, aiming to watch your cookies crumble, like never before, I really want you and a whole lot more, for sure, there's no cure for this love, It's a bug, don't scratch it, chill baby and relax it, while I penetrate, butt in the air, face up no sound, its going down, until I'm empty, round two what you going to do, reload and pop off, get naked take your top off, allover again, baby we living in sin, your love inspires me to win.

K. Gotti

HALF BLOOD TIES

I don't blame you for my Bro's death~ cause its the Qadar, but you was my rappy and you aint keep it gutter, same pop different mothers, but I always treated you like my brother, showed you love like no other, how you let the game become us, and left me for dead, I always shared my bread, and still I remain loyal, even when the temperature boils, tried to put you on when I passed off the oils, that NY connect, no job but I gave out checks, I'm the opposite of the rest, and one of the livest from out the west, I struggle trying pass the test, plus my status is rare, I got faith so I'm bounce back like Brittney Spears, situation still the same cause nobody cares, you cats are lost, I was 12 years old considered a boss, giving orders, no restaurant, but serving trays, no bleek but I'm coming of age, read the story, don't skip the page, no afro puffs but you see my rage.

K. Gotti

Faithful

I just wanna be faithful, and lower my gaze, like the summertime, blocking the heat with the dark shades, us being partners in a game of spades, not young no more, its like we coming of age, I plan to perform, rather on the street, or on stage, love is difficult, sort of like a maze, don't stop reading the book, keep turning the page, I'm attracted to your lips, plus the hair on your legs, even the toes, I plan to suck those, yours will be the first, sucking the clit will quench my thirst, and when I'm done, put everything back in reverse, and whoever did you wrong, I consider them jerks, cause your the loving type, that's what makes me wanna do right, but if I fall short, don't judge me, I rather you kiss me and hug me, and tell me you love me, treat you like coming to America, and lay down the rose petals, its like I won the race, and you was the medal, even though I'm deening, I'm still rustling with my demons, now that's major, still gotta deal with the haters, all I got for them, is a can of raider, they can get it now or later.

K. Gotti

NO JUSTICE

Can't blame Barack for the crooked cops, they don't honor the badge, all they respect is the cash, anyone will do in front of the judge, the internal affairs won't budge, a lot of contraverse, 10 to 20 years the DA trying hurt me, Falsely accused, family missing me so there being abused, that means we both lose, guilty as charged, a few more years of walking the yard, appeal pending, there's no ending, to the just-us-system, everybody's a victim, not playing the race card, Black & Hispanic are the only ones behind bars, No Justice No Peace, corrupt officers patrolling the streets, when is it going to cease, not until they start telling the truth, they trying to bury our youth, racially profiled for rocking a gold tooth, or driving a fancy car, no matter if you work or your a star, They don't care who you are, from NY to PA, or world wide, police brutality is still on the rise, from Martin Luther King I had a dream to Rodney King, and Sean Bell, they don't give out free lunches only free shells, no questions asked, Fire 'em and take they Badge.

K. Gotti

Success Over Fame

Baby I'm loving your style, we going come off like Kevin & Tiffany Chiles going the whole eight miles, so act like a cool aid pack and smile, sometimes I laugh to keep from crying, and I ask myself is living better than dying, who knows, I might be lying, but damn if I aint trying, no wings but I'm still flying, private jets I wanna cash million dollar checks, dreams are sky's the limit, I want it all, so I'm continue to try to get it, even though a lot of folks would hate to see me with it, but who cares, I did 11 years, and counting, the type of money I'm aiming for, I'll need a accountant, to keep tabs, I'm in the cut, but still on Bill Gates ass, always broke bread from my stash, now the cash aint green no more, too many dudes acting like whores, came along way from doing chores, I'm trying make the Forbes, top ten, and move for ten, and the pen, no I don't twitter, trying own my own business like Dean Witter.

K. Gotti

AMERICAN DREAM

I got a million dollar hand, without touching the game, that's why lames stay in one lane, while I switch my bitch like I switch my chain, stay cocky, why the feds watch me, still on my feet even though I took a beaten like Rocky, cats hate so they mock me, get that pure work from poppi, a lot of cats will never be rich, so stop dreaming, I take bodies like weebay, you niggaz soft like Neeman, flow so nice the hoes be fieneing, talking about they knocked up, I'm like how when you swallowed the semen, Betrayal is worst then death, I play the horse in these streets like a game of chess, aim for the head not the chest, still alive so I must be blessed, only got love for kin folk fuck the rest, and I'm a Big Fella, when I spit I make 'em sick like salmonella, team tight the opposite of Rocka Fella, love to my Bro and the Rest of the Team, far from Mike Jones but I'm living the American dream.

K. Gotti

Money Bags

No doubt I'm riding on this caper, blood line is green I'm addicted to the paper, the ones with big faces, team in all black imitating the matrix's, season vets leaving no traces! meaning evidence, look who I'm riding wit its evident, all soldiers Gorilla backs, 3 glocks one sk we stay strapped, rated R this shit action pack, no movie, real facts of life no Tootie, we aint come for the sex only the Booty, one false move get smacked with the tool, nothing personal just business, ski mask no need to kill the witness, hold up I hear movement in the kitchen, no its the cat I'm tripping.

If your name wasn't mentioned, that means you wasn't worthy, I ball hard like James Worthy, I aint bite my tongue you niggaz heard me, I'm counting this paper so don't disturb me, to much loyalty you deserve me, Its hate in your blood real killers out now come get it in blood, two middle fingers up no kisses and hugs, death to all plugs thinking you thugs, real cats Hilly, FB, and all the above, I don't speak about dudes I don't know cause there's no love, yeah I'm taking shots so take these slugs, free of charge, a million for the defense so my whole squad get discharged.

K. Gotti

LETTER TO MY BROTHER

Two years passed and the pain is still there, everyday I'm still wishing you was here, Lost granny, poppop, and Aunt Jose, and Mars so the tears are still there, No one knows what tomorrow will bring or even next year, Death is a part of life even if it ain't fair nobody looks out for mommy, How could you expect them to care, Hopefully I'll be home soon, after 10 long years and family still ain't family I get more love from my peers, Meeka and Marg look out for your seeds as though they were theirs, out here its like a jungle, I gave the game up no longer passing out· bundles its Books, Clothing Lines, Movie scripts everything from the muscle, whoever thought your brother would switch up his hustle, and a change gonna come, cause Gotti said, When they took your life it was like Gotti bled, Nowadays you gotta struggle to survive, and on these streets its hard trying to stay alive, And our new president is black, can you believe that, and people still only love you when your winning, Lost a whole lot but I'm still grinning, And by me still breathing, there's not a day that goes pass, I don t think about making it even, But if something goes wrong what are the chances of the family grieving, I wasn't there to watch Lil Lib start teething, this is the end of my letter Bro, and I don't even know the reason.

Letter to my Brother

K. Gotti

Fantasy

Waiting to exhale no Whitney, this is real love
no fairy tales, toe fetish, peel off hundreds like
I'm slicing lettuce, Chocolate and Strawberries,
nipples covered by Cherry's loving the
mustache, and how the legs are so hairy,
reservation's at the Marriott order room
service, anything you want I'm at your service,
our body's custom fitted, bend over let me fit
in, arched back booty in the air, pause for a
minute cause I'm in there, G-spot, your
goodies are hot, summer warm, tree top, cold
beverage, hold you by the waist side use it as
leverage, until I reveal the surprise, my face
knee deep in between your thighs, multiple
orgasms, vibrating like a back spasm, wet towel
therapy, this love is the remedy, message the
clit, tongue work, while your bones jerk from
the climax, spilled milk, skin soft as silk, your
fancy, its just my Fantasy.

K. Gotti

Single Parent

Everyone talking about single ladies, just take care of those babies, I was born in the seventies far from a eighties baby, my own best company cause cats are shady, single parent home my mom raised me, the best way she could, no way out, trapped in the hood, never lived in the projects, so it's all good, now welfare that's another story, three bedroom row house, two story, kerosene heaters, a few notches from Hurricane Katrina, no flood, roaches and bugs, one income so who are you to judge, even rats and mice, come too far to turn back, so I continued to live life, over the years it got a whole lot better, more work and more cheddar, vacation spots enjoying the weather, but never can I forget the struggle, no childhood I was forced to hustle, just so my family could manage, this is the outcome with one Single Parent.

K. Gotti

A Change Gonna Come

They say a change gonna come, But I can't tell, not giving up cause I'm determined to prevail, mom still in the struggle I'm still in jail, Back against the wall like what if all fails, I'm not trying go back to the drugs and scales, I just need one more chance without real, to exercise my skills, they call me Road Runner the way I'm chasing these mills, this is slavery just minus the field, trying move my family up in the hills, my Brother died in the streets like Romelo's Brother on Sugar Hill, And they want me to chill, But somebody gotta pay the bills, so I aim for the Book deal, In this industry I'm Steven Segal Hard to Kill.

K. Gotti

No Way Out

No matter how many times I change my thoughts. my brain reflects back to what I was taught, aim for the win by all means, I guess hustling is embedded in my genes, I'll do it with out a team, the game over my dreams, goals are side tracked, can't get the monkey off my back, no time to relax, trying push brand new Cadillac's, or the Bentley coupe, bricks of raw, or that Shag diesel no hoops, razor blade glass plates, not a shark more like a bathing ape, feed me hundred dollar bills, don't need Bananas or grapes, Ben Franklin traits, just a different color, under the same umbrella, not raining, but drops of drizzle's, balling without double dribble, free throws missing the basket, its either get rich or die broke in a casket, you dudes left me for dead in jail you rotten bastards when it was only crumbs I was asking, for a small defense, only to prove my innocence.

K. Gotti

Changing Faces

Stop acting other then yourself, you didn't get that way until you accumulated some wealth, I'm the same rather broke or rich, same dude you use to hug the block with and pitch, and the same one who got knocked and didn't snitch, why no help when you hood rich, don't bring the fake tears when I'm laying in a ditch, it's death without a kiss, and I aint mad at you like pac, no job but still on the clock, never wore a mask, how could you forget the same one who gave your girl the cash, to put on your books, two hood cats living the lives of crooks, I put my life on the line, bringing that coke back across state line, and still no love after doing a dime, It's your turn now so enjoy your shine, there's no hate, I feel I deserve a slice off your plate, only cause I broke bread when I had it, you drove all my cars the stick and the automatics, even supporting our drug habits, But I continued to maintain, I'm still stuck in that mind frame, Death B-4 Dishonor, all I know is Loyalty, Trust, and Honor.

K. Gotti

ABUSIVE LOVER

And she's your kids mother, you rather beat her then kiss and hug her, you are a abusive lover, with no respect for your own mother, and we paint that picture, its true love going get ya, I was young and witnessed my mom being abused, couldn't grasp on which way to move, too young to have something lose, this is the life we choose, true facts, don't mean to be rude, no different from Ike and Tina, lives torn apart, we put this separation between us, no longer together like Martin and Gina, going to school trying better myself, your jealous thinking I'm out there selling myself, but that's not the case, dark glasses to block the bruise on my face, I need a good man to take your place, and you blame it on the alcohol and drugs, but that's a lie, you love making me cry, I gotta get away from this Abusive Relationship, cause I don't wanna die, love keeps me coming back, thoughts are scattered so how can I relax, friends telling me to leave that's the best payback, but starting over is a great setback, he begs for one more chance, and I think all we have is each other, Don't fall for it Baby girl, it won't stop 'em from being a Abusive Lover.

K. Gotti

Team Player

We should've been friends to the end fuck chuckie, I seen both of us getting rich parting chicks like Bootz and Bucky, how you feel you can't trust me, our beef was a major topic, we played on the same team like Tracy McGrady Skip to my Lou Houston Rockets, this bullshit beef gotta stop it, I'm doing 10 to 20, why you at the lot trying cop it, Benz coupe should've dropped it, try tucking your pride, so I can give you the real that'll overshadow the lies, Before one of us dies, over the he say she say, that's dudes acting like broads, they riding with the feds doing what they want, thinking they above the law, my whole bid I stood tall, I don't have no picks I'm talking to all yaw, I played friendly without ice cream, Just me being loyal to my team, something people don't respect got me chasing cats for small checks, when I shouldn't want for nothing, over a decade you dudes still stuntin, I'm riding solo without the K, I'm the same from when I use to trap on the J, I never changed my Jersey, color still green, like Paul Pierce, my kind is rare, I always been fair, never a cross artist, passed checks around like spalding, no bouncing moving books now, no ounces.

K. Gotti

A Dedication

Whoever said death was pretty, come here kitty kitty, you aint the only one who misses titty, a real dude who always stayed shitty, from the ave to the state penn and Brook, two hood cats living the life of crooks, I read your words in the obituary, heartfelt and a little tenderly, But I understand you lost a friend & husband I lost my man, only if he was here to see my vision, how my life style changed in prison, book writer, rapper and entrepreneur, bread winner for sure, I really loved dude to the core, I seen us taking trips off shore, me, you, him and a female I adore, look how fast the plan changed, living life in the fast lane, fancy whips big chains, he was there for me when the cats I grew up with started frontin, he sent me money orders in bunches, It's like we knew each other from the days of free lunches, he kept it real when he was munching, the opposite I'm just waiting for a break, Just so I can make it even, his mom ain't the only one grieving, a lot of people died for no reason, these are signs of the hour, love, fear, hope, power, all I got is the good and bad memories, so I'm hold on to them like he was kin to me.

K. Gotti

Violated Trust

Got me turning in my sleep, not knowing when the feds going creep, had to learn sign language, cause you dudes are out of order, taking the feds orders, long Bid no money orders, expecting the hood to support us, my daughter's mom is your wife, with fame comes a price, violated trust over a couple of bucks, this segregation aint us, It's not white & black It's the money and crack, CI informants and wire taps, kidnappers and carjackers, ex-con turned rappers, the whole world is a stage, Indictment's more then one page, don't know who's telling, it's their soul they're selling, just to remain free, to continue to win, new tires but the wheels don't spin, four letters life inside the pen, new chapter in my life so I'm married to the pen, trying to find out when the unfaithfulness is gonna end, no Diane Lane I'm going insane, can't stay ahead of the game, so many new faces, CBS missing without traces, long record multiple cases Kinfolk lives are tuff, no help from my man only violated trust.

K. Gotti

BROKEN SYSTEM

Lost alot behind these bars, I don't have a 150
on my face; I got invisible scars, I was the head
of my household like Charles in charge, tired
of playing cards and walking the yard,
dominoes and chess tables, $16.5.0 a month
for cable, those that are able, 19¢ an hour,
eight men in a shower, no respect just power,
in chow lines fighting for bigger portions, I'm
just thankful I'm not an orphan, still on tilt
about my baby mom getting an abortion,
Decade in prison for chasing a fortune, can
never make up for my misfortune's, Been shot
down a million times over, no matter what still
didn't fold over, never understood the cold
shoulder, learned alot I'm much older, I
thought I told ya, that I won't stop, drive still
the same just minus the block, falsely accused
by dirty cops, and I still hold my head high,
shot down for pre-release, cause they think I'm
a goon plies, ear plugs 24/7 to block out all the
lies, did all my programs, so damn if I aint try,
how many more years of hearing the babies cry,
I don't know so I ask why.

K. Gotti

To The Top

Brought you a gift and I wrapped it myself! I'm so hot, its like battling myself, most dudes are like old books, stacked on a shelf, and I want the title, I don't look up to nobody, I'm my own idol, blew trial, but never put my hand on the bible, its a helluva life, I wouldn't trade it in, if I had to think twice, I'm married to the game, plus I gotta wife, all natural, nothing under the knife, connected like Bob Barker, so the price is right, and its to the top, until the casket drop, give you a rush card, so you can shop, no more auctions, everything off the lot, why not?, that's the question, everything I get is a blessing, Muslim so you'll never catch me in church confessing, trying bring my family out the recession, mom's weak so I know she's stressing, I didn't need 9 years to learn my lesson, back out with changed habits, trying make the trip to magic city to push the line, TM, come back straight to the lot cop the BM, meeting with Damon John, gotta see him.

K. Gotti

I'M DIGGING YOU

No doubt getting head on the beach, that's a treat, and I return the favor I want us to be closer then neighbors, in this life it's nothing greater, every time I see you, you sharp as a razor, and I like your style, baby you drive me wild, from your kiss, to your hips, I wouldn't mind having you served on a dish, and I'm lick the plate, now desert that's when things start to escalate, all night long never taking a break, you being my wife, is a chance I'm willing to take, the good and the bad, your still the best I ever had, even though I mentioned that in my last rhyme; I think you should know that all the time, and its only right that you're mine, I gotta use my words wisely, I want our family to be tighter then the Isley, and all the BS I put that behind me, picture me letting the lames out shine me, it'll never happen, that's like JayZ retiring from rapping, at the top of his game, so ready for a change, I can taste success, baby I'm at my best, just trying be patient, while enduring this test, and hope I'm able to answer the three questions, when I'm put to rest.

K. Gotti

Homerun

Never played baseball, but its the 9th inning, baby it may look like I'm losing, but I'm still winning, same street cat, just minus the sinning, I want us to bring that beat back to the beginning, like we never strayed apart, and I couldn't be mad at ya cause I remember when you played your part, missed you when you was gone, so your love was in my heart, never shed a tear, cause they were invisible, without you a dude was real miserable, its like you didn't take my feelings more considerable, every time spent with you was memorable, true story, you can never bore me, that's why I don't forget that much, and I'm that man you can trust, loving you is like dope, when you get that rush, and looking at you is the opposite of hallucinating, without that dust, in my eyes is 11 years of lust, for you cuttie, that's why I couldn't take my eyes off your booty, and I plan to show love to Tyree and Smoodie.

K. Gotti

Just Venting

I'm a boss, so I expect more, I prefer ladies, fuck whores, and when I get mad, I vent more, I aim for the win, cause I want more, why settle for less, when I'm ranked one of the best, no doubt this is a test, won't stop trying win, until I'm put to rest, if you cant stand the heat, baby I understand, this what you get, when you got Gotti as your man, I ain't never been a groupie, but I always been one of your fans, that's why I asked for your hand, in marriage, lets do it without the carrots, I plan to get rich like the Hilton's, money longer then Paris, lifestyles lavish, its not about the fashion, its just my· passion, to aim for the top, 2012 Porsche, are the Rolls Royce dropped, I'ma done with trying put my money together just to cop, the game is over, the blocks to hot, and I'm go at anybody, for the number one spot, in that industry, what I care ain't none of them kin to me, if they was, it still wouldn't matter, I'm serving foes and family on death platters.

K. Gotti

In Memory Of My Brother

You left this earth without seeing your son, or meeting my oldest daughter, the clock is still ticking for some, the rest are out of order, Lil Lib and Reema are cool, Mom dukes is the supporter, a lot done changed, except for my situation still cuffed in chains, it's a 100 to 1 outnumbered by the lames Nert got murked; and Diddy passed away, that's three good fellas who use to rep the J, 10 years in that's to long to stay, I wrote a few books hoping that'll pave the way, you know their classics cause I got a whole lot to say, trying to make it home boy I cant wait for that day, me and Khay are back on good terms, and I'm taking allergy pills cause I'm allergic to the worms, Meeka in recovery for stomach pains mixed with infectious germs, Joe the boss is back out from the pen, Stafakhan just went back in, for making rookie mistakes, cats don't know what to do when they catch a break, and I can still recognize the real from the fakes, I take the bitter with the sweet, like give and take, your baby boy will be four this year, just wish you was here to cut the cake, even though that's something I don't celebrate, that's me keeping it real, good dudes always catch raw deals, I'm out Bro until it's my turn to play the field.

K. Gotti

Lady Boss

Call you Lady Boss, the other chicks lost,
make'em craw back inlines, like a glass mirror
with that raw, you deserve a real nigga cause
you stand tall, just don't fall, but if you do I'll
pick up the pieces, close mouth when the law
try to impeach us, your mobbed in, like mob
wives different breed, moving at a fast speed,
untouchable minus the greed, we got kids to
feed, and family members, the real is in us,
unrehearsed but protective over our turf, we
should've been tight since birth, a new
beginning, and baby we winning, even with the
odds against us, as long as we don't let nobody
twist us, stay focused it's a big picture, and
brilliant vision, just need backing, lets get it
like Goldy without the macking, mommy the
versus are hot but I aint just rapping, I'm
hustling without trapping, the fans are
applauding that's why they clapping, even the
haters who thought it couldn't happen, Five
star vacation resorts relaxing, trips to a foreign
land, everything blew up from a small plan,
keep pushing no limit, no matter what I do I
put my heart and soul in it, so I can win it,
even with a loss, still call you lady boss, until
the end of time, baby we both going shine,
through the darkest of clouds, so pat yourself
on the back and take a bow, bond tight
without walking down the aisle.

K. Gotti

FAMILY AFFAIR

Get well it's going be the coldest winter ever, no sistah souldjah, we been family since we were kids, we just got older, your not leaving this earth until it's your turn, I thought I told ya, a family affair, God willing I'll be home next year, and even though we aint twins, we look just alike, green eyes complexion light bright, or yellow like tweety bird, I love you kinfolk you heard, all I got is my word, I'll never break it, real til the death I'll never fake it, I'm just waiting for your recovery praying, you make it, gotta live life before it's taking, I'm still doing my thing history in the making, minus the setbacks, I see me pushing that Maserati jet black; like a hawk, disloyal people like Denzel did Ethan Hawk, but our bond could never be broken; I'll always be here for you I'm not joking, A family of five plus five tokens, small bus fare, you always treating me fair, and showed me love cause you cared, I wish I was there, by your side, but hold your head and do it in stride, with my last breath I'ma ride, and if I strike rich I'm share, cause it's a family affair.

K. Gotti

MIND BLOWN

Never thought about tuition, all I knew was a coffee pot baking soda ice cubes in the kitchen, down south was trapping I was pitching, anything to palm my mittens, without gloves, so crack in my system, most of my life been in the system, didn't give it any thought. What's the chances of me getting caught, lawyer money no bail, wiretaps on the cell, the PCP messing with my brain cells, on top of the syrup and pills, riding dirty until someone gets killed, DUI or a senseless drive by, not with the gangs or the colors, just another dead brother, who cares nobody, pullout the white sheet to cover up the body, lives lost at a rapid speed, can't control your anger so the guns you squeeze stop and think for a minute put the pistol at ease cameras flash but no one says cheese, so the picture it's blurry, eyes puffy from the tear drops, but nobody's crying, can't trust a lot people too much lying, black spot in the circle, who's pointing the finger, Spanish chick same mind frame as ginger, Sammy without casino, Tony Montana Scarface Al Pachino, fish scale, complexion change lighter tone, nose bleeding mind blown.

K. Gotti

Never Forgotten

Fifteen years later, you still aint forgotten, aint nothing change, just different young bulls on the corner clocking, and the dudes we knew all our lives are still rotten, I know you cant hear me but what's popping, and I aint balling like Big Willie, one thing for sure I miss Billy, still aint find real love like Chilli, its only a few left with the same caliber as Hilly, No matter what still Repping Philly, city of Brotherly Love, although most hate, a lot of my relationships been worse than Hell's date, no b.e.t, but I had a few bad chicks come see me, road for a minute and fell off, who cares I'm still Gotti the West Philly Boss, even after a million times over of taking a loss, who said the game didn't cost, I still remember us eating rice and gravy quarter hugs with duck sauce, eventually we graduated to syrup and tuinal, and that's when everything went wrong, and caused your death, I wear that everyday its embedded in my chest; even behind bars I aint settling for less, you was more then a friend you was the best; that always had my back; a live wire how real is that, and who can take your place, when you was my ace, now I'm caught up cause I let the lames invade my space, without my permission, so the law wants to put me out of commission, but I'm still fighting cause I don't know about quitting, or stopping; still missing you Homey but you'll never be forgotten.

K. Gotti

UNTIL THE DEATH OF ME

I'm fight to the death, I'ma give you everything I got even my last breath, with my free will to past the test, everything comes in stages, A small book that can hold a thousand pages, mind frame is amazing, trapped in the belly of the beast, in the law library twice a week, anything to hit those streets, except for selling my soul, that goes for those cats who told, swagger on a million plus cocky and bold, stand up dude that's the title I hold, but the lames wanna see me die ln jail so my body can mold, they shouldn't count their chickens, even though their agenda's are hidden, locked in the closet, no R. Kelly, cats dropping dimes like Kane on Belly, I'm in a dorm setting 8 cellies, but still a RN, not an registered nurse, Raw Nigga since my birth, giving these marks Hell on Earth, kinfolks ride hard cause they know my worth, and I'm hood no ace, but no doubt I hustle hard, buy it soft and make it hard, pop whip it, that's the stretch, I need extra cake for whatever I invest, and the loyalty and trust is a must, until I'm draped in oil that IceBerg or that China Musk, still down from that 2001 drug bust, 10 rappy's but I'm the only one standing, so the bank roll I'm demanding, time well spent, the message has been sent, dark shades no tent, and it's a whole lot left in me, that's the real until the Death of Me.

K. Gotti

The Real 56th Street

I really be 56th street, so what you fakes gotta say to me, I got a dime in for the block, drugs and conspiracy, and it's only a few more who Rep as hard as me, their either dead or locked in the box, I did a stretch, I aint run to the cops, real man to my family nothing like my pops, I'm on the low waiting for my shot, at the title, I'm the hood's idol, so respect it, yaw bow out when the game get hectic, I ride with no brakes, middle finger to you fakes, I only get what I take, you undercover Fag's, and rats hiding behind a mask, you niggas make me wanna gag, I'm talking throw up, hold your breath cause Gotti about to blow up, a million ventures, I aint talking great adventures, more like a road map, keep standing on the corner selling those packs, while I imitate YC stacks on top of stacks when yaw going to burry the hate, I'm on roller blades now, and I cant even skate, its been along time coming, don't start running, or hiding go in your stash and start dividing, that's simple math, no coke all cash, a lot of frauds in the game wont last, I'm who the courts wanna defeat how when I'm the real 56th Street, and I'm still grinding without the block, time still running so watch the clock.

K. Gotti

Undeniable

5'2 thick in the waist, no doubt cute in the face, lame's get out of pocket have me catch a new case, we on a private island leaving no trace, not a red bone, she's sexy chocolate no sprinkles, I just wanna taste her get to the middle, do a tongue search, I'm really happy she's on this earth, I'll take her in a pair of pants or a short mini skirt, but how do I get pass the marriage and children, my thoughts about her are pass the ceiling, I aint trying to buy her she's worth more then a million, body like a murder scene its making a killing, plus nice hands and pretty feet, that's a treat, the total package, There's nothing she's lacking, except a RN Real Nigga, and I don't mind waiting, you gotta be patient for greatness, I'm thinking to myself how can they hate this, Real feeling's no fake shit, more then a dime shorty is the Ish, don't care about basketball wives Shawnie & Tammi, my heart aches for Lil Pammy, us in front row seats at the Grammy's, living like stars, still Repping the hood from the battle scars, and I trust she's reliable and no doubt undeniable.

K. Gotti

YOU LOST ME

Having you around was like three's company, gave you a million ideas so you could start the company, because in reality wasn't nobody helping me, to much pressure you couldn't hold it, still don't understand why you fold it, treating you like clay I tried to mold it, but it's over, and I'm still carry the jail on my shoulders, I'm me rather in a Benz or a Rover, mind frame is sober, no drugs or drinks, counting this paper helps me think, I wrote letters until I ran out of ink, they didn't want me to win they wanted me to sink, too much ambition, did the time cause I couldn't see myself snitching, bills gotta get paid plus tuition, I needed a Betty Shabazz cause she didn't do no bitching, stood by her man when it got hot in the kitchen, I just wanted you to listen, hear me out, not Mexican but a helluva route, all pertaining to winning, and nothing to do with sinning, I knew you were a square, you said you would ride for a deuce, but you didn't give me a year, I don't think it was fair so many lies, I was with you when Daddy made you cry, us against the world, you left me for Earl, or whatever his name is, I just hope he's the right one for your kids, I had plans on handling my biz, did you know I was a genius or better yet a wiz, but it's to late you lost me, and that's free so it didn't cost me.

K. Gotti

FROM ME TO YOU

You can most def take the number 1 spot, your a ride or die chick, plus I'm your daughter's pop, that makes us tighter then ants twat, if we riding it has to be until the casket drops, Ball hard and shop to we drop, nothing's impossible, I'm working hard to get past the obstacles, on top of that we got history, stay down don't be a mystery, I need loyalty & trust, love comes last, I learned that from those disloyal chicks in the past, no doubt I wanna jump in that ass, thick or thin, I got a dime in the pen, unmarried sex is a sin, and never do you have to lie, I'm the real so keep your eyes on the prize, and I'm worth the wait, I'ma big fish all you gotta do is bite the bait only the one above knows our fate, I just need a break; So I can make it happen; all I do is win, I ain't good with rappin, I leave that to the plugs, and those, wanna be thugs, M.O.B., Money Over Bullshit, that's the green with a twist, I'm not Santa Claus but I got a big list, this is from me to you, we partners in crime so let's make it do what it do.

K. Gotti

Single Ladies

I like Keisha and Val, plus who doesn't want a bad chick with cash, as well as a Bunny with a Black girls ass, everybody's cheating, Keisha is having fun but damn is she freaky, Val's confused white man or a black dude, A failed five year relationship has her afraid to choose, April has jungle fever married with no children, on the brink of divorcing, For being unfaithful with the mayor, Darryl is hurt thinking how could she betray us, Omar is gay and I aint talking about happy, no different from the wire, different characters with the same agenda,Christina is a fashion roast, but she won over Val that's why they popped a toast, someone's keeping secrets from college, something kinky that Val didn't want to acknowledge, it was more then just a man giving that poompoom a Polish, a female was tossing her salad, Darryl wants revenge plus greed, trying take all of April's cheese, leave that trust fund empty, like his heart, the infidelity broke the spark, Single now so they mingle, with rich men, some average, Keisha wants Malcolm plus his jewels, I'm talking carrots, Val's independent make up sex with her ex still couldn't mend it, April still searching to pick up the pieces, after hiring a lawyer, while Omar is still man chasing, and Christina running around with the professor, when she should be looking for a stylist to dress her, no matter if they watch movies or play bingo, it's still three women single.

K. Gotti

Hate It Or Love It

You gotta tuck your pride, if we going ride like Bonnie & Clyde, It's do or die, get money and stay fly, as long as we alive, let the past be the past and get this cash; and if I'm out of town we can skype, look how fast things change you no longer gotta write, that's the lifestyle you live being Gotti's wife, not in the ring but I'm the fighting type, I'm the shit, those other cats are hype, or better yet over rated, I'm the most hated, cause I move out, I'm still repping Philly even living in the south, I don't want the fame or the clout, Its not worth it, to much pain and suffering, but it all comes with hustling, no matter what field, get rich and chill, go to trial or take the deal, lets make our bond tight like Heidi Klum and Seal, I'm just keeping it real, and I'll never betray your trust, same face no nip tuck, loyalty over the buck, it last longer, our relationship has potential to grow stronger, so hate it or love it, we can't put the bullshit above it.

K. Gotti

RAW DEAL

Cops pulling capers on camera , another innocent victim locked in the slammer, the judge don't care he still slams the hammer, Jeff Cujdik and Reynalds, these cases ain't piling up coincidental, too much time messing with my mental, got me seeing the psych, not guilt but still paying the price, married to the life, without throwing the rice, everyday I wake up I'm rolling the dice, until I crap out, in the law library until I'm let out researching cases, poker hand straight aces, a lot of people getting set up different races, it really doesn't matter who pays the cost, the victim and the family both take a loss, another Raw Deal, same mentality as Macky just minus the shield, can't afford to go to trial, so I'm copping the deal, can't sleep at night so I'm popping the pills, suicide watch, I'm just keeping it real, true facts far from being surreal, this is major ordeal, crooked cops still playing the field, until they reach their quota, switched the task force around and the corruption still ain't over, no justice no peace a million obstacles to get to the streets, dealt a raw hand, still fighting like Ed Lover and Dre on who's the man.

K. Gotti

We Fly

Two birds of a feather flock together, we above average, two carrots two birds yellow parrots, private jets flying around Paris, no clothes we shop when we land, 100 acres we own our own land, trips to Brazil to sun tan, middle fingers to you haters, you work for us now so pay us, income tax, baby we rich so relax, no need to work hard, we flying above the stars, but still holly hood living amongst the stars, success ain't make us change, we brought the whole family a Range, it is what it is when you're o-deing in change, your whole lifestyle change, a different lane from the lames, longevity with a perfect aim, first class if we take a plane, everything served on trays, no window shopping or layaways, this ain't back in the day's, don't know Fonz but these are happy days, let's celebrate, years of celibate, Disney World play a bit, all in fun, I'm a son of a gun, diamonds the same color as the sun, off shore account if I'm ever on the run, and I ain't gotta lie, what can I say but we fly.

K. Gotti

I'MA BOSS

I'ma Boss either broke or rich, I dont have the city flaming cause I aint snitch, I just was hugging the block trying get rich, it took incarceration for me to find my nitch, started writing so quickly my hustle switched, so many lives lost to that casket and that project bench, until it's my turn, I'ma rep my own swag, black on black Jag, welcome home like Frank, brown suit case filled with franks short for big faces, no address, on the move a million locations, stay off the air waves learned that in the basics, drug deals in the stair cases, condos no elevators, but my status elevated, funny how I'm the most hated, even behind the wall, on the bench until it's my turn to ball, even humpty dumpty took a fall, Born different I walked before I crawled pappi got 'em for cheap get 'em delivered in a U-haul, move them all before the fall, I'ma need a saw, so I can break bread, with my kinfolk and friends, never been stingy with my ends, I prefer the Maserati over the Benz, I hope my good deeds outweigh my sins, a lot of hard work to accumulate these ends, blood sweat and tears, young soul but still ahead of my peers.

K. Gotti

When It All Falls Down

When you winning you get shown mad love, lots of chicks and friendly hugs, passenger side is your man, but he's known as a scrub, late nights end of the Dove, we don't even use the bed, better sex on the rug, one night stand just because , bubble baths in the Jacuzzi tub, my main broad sweeps it under the rug, because I'm an athlete, so I get free treats, until I was hit hard by cancer, now I cant get a lap dance from a dancer, no scholarship, I'm down in the pits, hospital bill has mother in the ditch, part time caterer, full time bar tender, so many different things on the agenda, gotta fight back cause I'm a contender, girl don't know me no more she's a pretender, in my heart I'm still a winner, ambition on a hundred, where did all my friends go they didn't keep it one hundred, music plays loud but still can't hear the sound, nobody's around, weight loss like a crack addict, working out again I'm back at it, small weights, a few months to live, and still no break, this is the outcome when you take things for granted, a lot on the plate so you try not to panic, and the doctor said no more running, but that doesn't stop the let downs from coming, nor does it stop the birds from humming, and I can't take it laying down, from football to selling cars, came from a nobody to a star, until my foot stepped out of bounds, that's what happens when it all falls down.

Inspired by the movie:
All Things Fall Apart
by: 50Cent.

K. Gotti

Wandaring Confused

Addicted to Wandering, I think about you everyday so I spend my days pondering, on how our lives would be together, and what you and dude have was never he's cottage cheese, I'm Cheddar, your situation aint worse, but you can do better quality time spent like Chilli and Mayweather, I'm writing you a four page letter, just to let you know how I feel, in my heart this love is real, and do you feel the same, not drag racing, so its not a game, with love comes pain, why would I lie, I have nothing to gain, lets get married, you can keep your last name, cause I don't see no ring yet, I don't gamble, but I'm willing to bet, just don't leave me at the alter, like the girl did Hugh Hef, do you take her to be your wife? Yes, baby I'm the best, I'ma treat you like the host, he going to serve you like a guest, you deserve more, he going to give you less, I'll take the whole package that includes the nest, all you gotta do is fill in the circles, like a tabe's test, and if you pass I'll do the rest, even if it means taking chances, as long as my nights consist of romancing, every part of your body, do it in the back seat of the car or hotel lobby, make it last longer then Whitney and Bobby, please don't knock me til you try me, I'm talking refused, you are who I choose, Wandering over you confused.

K. Gotti

Out Of Sight Out Of Mind

Why yaw dudes aint breaking bread, I ain't dead, I'm trying look out for my folks, and my baby pretty Red, tired of hearing be patient and hold your head, I get that everyday from my old heads, yaw pass do on putting disloyalty to bed, but I'ma Rock on like a rock band, Kiss with a long tongue, you only respect looking down the barrel of a Devil's gun, the game is overrated cats killing for gum, and they don't send nothing to the jails, no neptunes but that's Fo'Real, and the disease is spreading like the ocean when the oil spilled, it's not only the hate it's the lies that kill, and they get mad at me for keeping it real, a whole lot of players at the table but no'one to deal, so that's when the cheating starts, I paid my dues and I played my part, the motivation keeps me sharp, young with a whole lot of heart, I'm the teacher giving out lessons Clark, or the principle, these rules are simple for criminals, and they love seeing us caged like animals, that's why they don't send a dime, cause you're out of sight out of mind.

K. Gotti

2012

Its no limit to how I rate you, you talking vacation I need a break too, Red dress Red bottoms, your a model, Red carpet for a idol, you hold that title, don't let nobody tell you different, every conversation I'm in your mentioned, just want you butt naked cooking in the kitchen, real nigga bad chick we together in the trenches, I got a story to tell just need you to listen, I wanna do everything for you without your permission, had a lot of women in my life but you're the only one that I'm missing, its both of your lips that I wish I was kissing, only if you could see my vision, the picture is painted so vivid, celebrate just to say we did it, its not hard to tell, I'm trying pull you out of that shell, ride with me baby Gotti going prevail, in or out of jail, real talk its not game I'm trying sell, keep your eyes open for 2012.

K. Gotti

A Decade Is Too Long

Over a decade is a long time a few years more than a dime and I need you here enjoying my time lonely nights is to much just to rollover I ask you when is it going to be over, tired of crying on my girlfriend's shoulder, not young anymore I'm only getting older a decade is such a long time,

When I first got knocked wasn't sure if you was going to ride, but you proved me wrong in due time, didn't know what I was facing for my new crimes, I remember seeing your face when the judge gave me a dime, I'm just keeping it real I'm not even trying to rhyme, they were all lies when you told me you were fine, you even tattooed my name on your thigh, on the visit I asked why? Your answer was one day you would be wifey. How is that when you don't even write me, I'm still breathing so my time didn't even expire, even Bartsdale made it home on the wire.

Over a decade is a long time a few years more than a dime and I need you here enjoying my time lonely nights is to much just to rollover I ask you when is it going to be over, tired of crying n my girlfriend's shoulder, not young anymore I'm only getting older a decade is such a long time,

Done with doing time behind bars, basketball/football Nelly the whole nine yards, and I can tell it's killing you softly, no warning you walked off softly, plus your kitty cat was on fire, you called the fire department to fulfill your desires, and I knew it would happen, chicks do anything when it starts scratching, first cat you ever rode a bid with, and the same dude you wanted to have kids with, that's the past like history, you don't respond to my cards, so I know you don't miss me, my swipe got hard when you use to kiss me, and I can't call your phone, nowadays you're laying with Tyrone, and what we had is gone,

Over a decade is a long time a few years more than a dime and I need you here enjoying my time lonely nights is to much just to rollover I ask you when is it going to be over, tired of crying n my girlfriend's shoulder, not young anymore I'm only getting older a decade is such a long time,

In Jail my name ring bells, stand up dude and I ain't tell, when I call home a lot of dudes are doing swell, doing anything to prevail, wire taps on the cell, I take what the game has to offer, turned down the plea the DA tried to offer, and took the judge head up, I would've respected you more if you would've told me you was fed up, no doubt I sit here telling myself it ain't fair, but who really cares, when it's only two months left in the year, ain't heard from you going on two years, debut should be next year, so cry me a river Brittney Spears,

Over a decade is a long time a few years more than a dime and I need you here enjoying my time lonely nights is to much just to rollover I ask you when is it going to be over, tired of crying n my girlfriend's shoulder, not young anymore I'm only getting older a decade is such a long time,

I rode six years out your dime, praying you come home soon so we both shine, but it didn't happen you ran out of time, and the love was so strong I'm sorry I did you wrong, and even though we never had sex, I still sent you boots and several checks, even put on the collect, plenty of nights in my bed crying, though you were locked up it felt like you was dying, or still running the streets, while I played with myself under the sheets, and I knew I had to move on, that's the reason I never told you I was going,

Over a decade is a long time a few years more than a dime and I need you here enjoying my time lonely nights is to much just to rollover I ask you when is it going to be over, tired of crying n my girlfriend's shoulder, not young anymore I'm only getting older a decade is such a long time,

Didn't even ask you to stand by my side, you chose to ride, the new modern day Bonnie and Clyde, wasn't really cut for the chase, I looked in your eyes and the expression on your face, don't even know if you went back to church like Mase, you didn't even check in to see if I was safe, undercover Holly Hunter without saving Grace, still appreciate the time you tapped in your safe, it's clear another nigga took my place, the way you went CBS missing without a trace, pre-release is around the corner and I'm still fighting my case, welcome home present like Mitch got from Ace.

K. Gotti

High Maintenance

Crystal body, she a hottie, canary yellow or two tone, who cares she's full grown, like a poodle, in a bad relationship with a noodle Ramen, but left the real cat hanging, while she parties at the playoffs, work extra hard never takes a day off, cause if you do then how can you expect a payoff, fired from the job thinking its only a layoff, a woman in the streets, freak in the sheets, I make the chic reach her peak, she's satisfied, orgasm mesmerized on cloud nine, shorty is a dime, Georgia Peach, sweet fruit, Dolce and Gabbana, gotta wine and dine her, top shelf Gucci belt, Monolo Blanik, Prada loafers, Maybach two chauffeurs, all black Testaroasta, Roberto Cavali, models in the alley, change clothes, platinum Handbone, high fashion thug passion, we dirty dancing, Seven jeans, ACG boots, Sean John, on the low, Rocawear and Polo, Mink Blanket, a 100 million for the taking, Timberland Chukkas, Versace, Luis Vuitton, Movado Rolex on the arm, Iceberg Coogi, Drunkn monky, Red Monky, no hood on the trunk, Red Phantom, Flying Spur, Fendi for sure, Dior Velour, Enyce Azzure, Yatcht off shore, private jets, flying over L.A.X., Giorgio Armani, old school Nautica and Tommy, Cartier wrist wear, Green Ice, over the top fast life, Christian LouBoutin, I'm a thug and a gentleman, Sunberry, plaid shirt Burberry, living swell bathing suit by Chanel, no patiance baby I'm high maintenance.

K. Gotti

FIGURE IT OUT

Why you still chasing waterfalls, I gave you several opportunities to be in the presence of a boss, the game is freaky all at a cost, so many noodles not enough sauce, I don't know if your repping the real or a cross, to many identities Rupaul, don't need no pity screw yawl put you on a auction block and trade off, to many schemes Madoff, your not on your job its like you laid off, and still trying reap the benefits from the payoff, that's wishful thinking, until everything in front of you deteriorates like a body stinking, your future ain't fading its sinking, right in front of your face, cause you don't know what part to play, and you still don't know your place, don't need you behind me, I need you face to face, plus on my side like track and field before they start the race, there's no timer but speed up the pace, before these doors open then its to late, cause everybody that's living aint destined for a break; I want you to ride with me but it's the bugs you gotta shake, try a new route, move you from the apartment into a new house, if you know Kareem then you should know what Gotti is about, just don't take to long to figure it out.

K. Gotti

I Heard It All Before

Keep talking about you can't wait to see me,
but some of you never climbed these
mountains, it's segregation, like in the 1950's
when they had Black and White water
fountains, only love I get is when I'm moving
ounces, and when I let those disloyal dudes
sleep on my moms couches, dudes always got
they hand out, I'm locked up still screaming
when they going let my man out, I rather see
my whole team on the streets, making moves
and making ends meet, and a hater is
something I never been, I been a boss I just
perfected my craft since I been in, moving at a
fast pace until I reach a dead end, cats eating
on the outside but they aint sending shit in,
and that's just history repeating itself, a lot of
people act new when they accumulate some
wealth, like they hit the lottery, and you
wonder why a broke cat got so many robbery's,
how can you feed your family on a McDonalds
salary, 8:50 a hour, I need money, Scarface can
have the respect and the power, and its hard
for a real dude to breathe when you
surrounded around cowards, prison have you
wearing extra clothes in the shower, just to
cover your Awarah, and I ask myself why don't
I care anymore, cause I heard it all before.

K. Gotti

OLD FRIENDS

Been friends since the second grade, both young around the same age, even graduated together from the fifth grade, after that its like we went our separate ways, you was doing you, I was caught up in the streets in the game, not knowing its a purpose for life not just the fame, and I know a lot of goons, but only one dude with the name Ricky Raccoon, we grew up fast skipping past the cartoons, even watched you on parking wars, wish I was home to stop the frivolous wars, since a lot of people set back and remained silent, like they was cheering on for the violence, at the end we all lost, real cats are going, only thing left is the frauds, so who wins even with a coin toss, plus we fought when we was younger, but we didn't let that deter us, we still remained brothers, nowadays the youngins are killing each other, in middle school we was known as the goodfellas, and the ladies man, I had the eyes you had the good hair, two fruits one apple one pair, a whole lot can change over the years, you was still around when I made bail from Rikers Island, the same night I lost my right hand man William Allen, yaw both left this earth in yaw sleep, a lot of people don't dig it but its deep, when your being wrapped in a white sheet, and who am I to hold a grudge, when all these years it was nothing but love, on top of that you got kids by my cuz, and one day we all will be judged, and I take my loss with my wins, just in memory of one of my old friends.

K. Gotti

SHORTY BAD!!

Shorty Bad hairy legs, sexy mustache, I'm attracted to her beauty and her nice ass, we aiming for the future we ain't looking in the past, Chanel and Dolce & Gabbana bags, every color, platinum Jag platinum umbrella, she on another level so what can you tell her, modern day Cinderella, chinky eyes mixed breed, seven digits that's what the numbers read, a lot of controversy fitting in those jeans, plus the shoe game is mean, racks on top of racks, all designs, special delivery never wait in line, Royal treatment for dimes, front pages of the New York Times, for looking good not for committing a crime, if it's up to me she going continue to shine, drink her like a bottle of wine, can't help myself she's one of a kind, I just want her to be mine, so I gotta work extra hard, so she'll have that Black card, free of charge, what can I say she's living large, on another level, lady's Rolex Iced Bezel, and I'm glad, cause shorty bad.

K. Gotti

Star Running Back

The hood think I ain't coming back, How? when I'm on the field like running back, black tar but I ain't running track, either the treadmill or the yard more then twenty laps, more then ten in a bundle we selling racks, four pies break it down all packs, you lames broke how yaw gonna relax, out of town money that's the best trap, shitting on you marks that's the best crap, riding two deep with the sk plus the mac, realness that's what you cats lack, I'm driving you on the passenger side of the Maybach, you still pitching I'm up next to bat, and I'm calling shots like the umpire how you like that, shopping sprees at Gucci you still doing TJ Max, credit cards and hundred grand all stacks; spend everything I'm trying max, from the first to the fifteenth I get it all back, yaw had silver spoons in yaw mouths I had to sell crack, still in the game star running back.

K. Gotti

Twelve Seventeen Still Remember You

Five years pass, and a lot has happened, Bree goes
to community college for acting, Delly's a
workaholic, but Bree's still balling with spalding,
Meeks out of the hospital but drawing, every
once and a blue I'm calling, a lot of cats are still
falling, rather by death or a cell block, can't run
to many crooked cops, they making it hard to
cop, Mom Dukes still looking for discounts when
she shop, ain't nothing change the same shit with
pops, Shakur crying poor, that's just a excuse to
get more, I can't get a check from those cats to
make it to the store, and Reema's being bad, Lil
Lib calls me Unc but he missing his Dad, I can't
cry but in my heart I'm still sad, I don't miss
what I don't got I miss what I had, my brother
my other half, Cece is still being her while Steph
gets suspended from class, life is short so don't
nothing last, I'm still chasing a fortune on
Russell Simmons ass, a lot of set backs, no
different from when I got left back, still came off
like Goldy from Mack, but I ain't trying go back
to that, legit paying tax, feed the family so we all
can relax, right now Marg has our back, and
that's a fact, and I'm working extra hard, for a
discharge, a lot of people started off small but
living large, I'm just chasing my dreams, never
will I forget that day of twelve seventeen.

K. Gotti

Back In The Day

When are we going make these dudes pay, bring back the hood respect like back in the day, man put me back on the J, the first block I made my own way, moving that P, sitting on the steps of mom P, bifocals glasses and still I can't see, my team nert, Diddy, Billy, Bert, Den and FB, can't forget J-rock, way before the dope and rocks, eight hour shifts no time clock, block party's but still open up shop, and neighbors felt safe, the same place I caught my first case, at thirteen with stacks in my safe, nowadays in the hood cats feel out of place, I don't know you cuz, I can't recognize your face, all you rookies breaking the rules, it's time to go back to school, of hard knocks, I birthed you lames so stop, knee deep in the game, even hustle in front of town watch, up with hope down with dope, cocaine whiter than the pope, real talk no joke, dedicated to the fienes, Wu Tang Clan all cream, water ice truck, I was all about a buck, even copped a few scooters, on the sideline a few shooters, like Desperado, got booked with my black mavado, can't see me Hallow man, I ain't got nothing else to say, just reminiscing back in the day.

K. Gotti

I Don't Need You

You got the game twisted, I'm not out there to
scratch the cat, when it starts itching, I'm the
real deal, my name has to be mentioned, yaw
didn't hold me down in the trenches, my folks
ride hard, and they don't do no bitching,
crying talking I don't have time, baby that's
fine, it's clear your not mine, I ain't ask you for
a dime, and you ain't ride the whole dime,
I'ma get my time to shine, like PO, and I'm get
that doe, hold the jails down, the lifers and the
ones on the row, how you put me on the back
burner, when I'm a earner, in so many ways,
came from a block that did 30 grand a day
back in the days, way before they was playing
with AK's, the game done changed, but not
me, I ain't begging no chick to come see me,
that's out the question, I'm young and restless,
not Victor Newman, or Keith Sweat, more like
Hugh Hef, all models, no hoodie rats, I'm
passed that so I need to move on, pack your
bags and get going, keep thinking I'm the
average, until I prove you wrong, I aint got
long, my ambition is strong, keep singing that
same old song, and I aint gotta break my neck
to please you, cause baby I don't need you.

K. Gotti

STRIPTEASE

Take everything off, except the heels, slow down sexy exercise your skills, I'ma make it rain all one hundred dollar bills, I ain't playing this is for real, this private session, is my therapy session, so don't keep me guessing, easy sliding down that pole, no sense in bruising that hole, I'm the director just play your role, bend down touch your toes, shake that apple bottom going raw dog no condom, I'm only playing, let me touch your hand, while the other one massage's my man, long nipples ooh warm milk, lay down on the mink quilt, spread eagle, let me do my research I'm a paralegal, and I'm guilty as sin, I'm ready to appeal, so I start sucking your toes just to give your body the chills, all I heard was soft moans, so I know that it's on, as I work my way up, she turned over on all fours, all I seen was her butt, she wanted a orgasm and I wanted a nut, two for the price of one, I wasn't no where near done, the body was crazy, I was trying give this girl a baby, I was a gentleman all night treating her like a lady, then I heard the knock at the door, who is this interrupting my time with a chick I adore, when it opened, I couldn't believe my eyes, but then it clicked, a surprise ménage, all I did was aim to please, this was the best one night striptease.

K. Gotti

Stay In Your Own Lane

Times have changed, stay in your own lane, your broke chasing fame, you're not a ladies man, your only a rappers fan, no common sense, everybody's, playing you're still on the bench, I gave you a yard, you only took an inch, crying cause you got pinched, hustling backwards, live your own life your not an actress, on a movie scene, on the other side the grass ain't always green, you're acting other than yourself now that you got a team, wake up it's only a dream, it's like you're lost, you listen to Rick Ross now you're a boss, lets keep it real, I went to trial I ain't take the deal, I'm just playing games twisting words, your a pack boy never seen a bird, and your lying you never keep your word, now you from New York you heard, Lupe Fiasco living like a star, where I'm going you can't see that far, somewhere up in the hills, the chick left cause you can't pay the bills, or even the car note, not even a comedian and your a joke, Kevin Heart, only larceny in your heart, I want the world to smell me like I farted, I don't even rap and the flow is retarded, not the president so no pardons, just the roast, everything I write is unrehearsed, you might look better in a hearse, in the way stealing out your girls purse, that's small change, I'll stop bringing the pain, as long as you stay in your own lane.

K. Gotti

RECESSION

I struggle just to pay my bills, college grad but still no jobs in my field, McDonald's is hiring I lack those skills, can't get medical insurance and the kids are ill, so I rob and steal, anything to make ends meet, not far from being kicked out on the streets, a lot of people around me, but I still feel alone in these streets, losing the fight but still no sign of defeat, recession hit home so the situation is deep, lips sealed so I can't speak, I'm starving I gotta eat, never played with needles but my body's weak, my chicks on the low trying creep, there's no hope, so I resort to old habits, cop the dope and bag it, no other choice, sore throat squeaky voice, house foreclosed, white substance in my nose, like Michele Pfiefer, nick rocks for the pipers, anything to rise back on top, so I'm back to the block, two for ones, welfare giving out access cards no ones, facing 25 years if I get caught with the guns, climbing in windows all black on like Run, nothing personal it's all about the funds, rescue me like Dennis Leary, the lifestyle I live is kind of scary, chasing worldly possessions, stil1 living outside my means in the recession, understand me clearly thru my confession, even with the hard times still thankful for the many blessings.

K. Gotti

Mind Racing

Mind racing 100 miles, I been thru a lot more then 100 trials, no concurrent sentence they ran it wild, can't hear you everybody talking loud, and I ain't deaf, you wasn't invited so why show up with the guest, I'm like a dog when he poops I make a mess, but focused on top of a little stress, a lot of shots being thrown so I rock the bullet proof vest, I'm just trying make it even, for my team that's locked up and the ones that stopped breathing, believe it or not they all deening, that means practicing Islam, I'm a made man, mob ties, like skinny Joey, you can't talk about me cause you don't know me, I'm as real as life, everything has a price, even your wife, so before you fall in love I would think twice, bucket full of cheese to feed the rats and the mice, not ace but everybody eats, even the fiends with no teeth, money long as my rap sheet, strictly ink on the paper, no longer letting the coke dry out on the paper, or using a razor, that's the outcome when the streets raise you, different ball game, only a few players, no help so the courts delay us, and I don't think it's fair, but who cares, it's stocks and bonds plus time shares, back and forth pacing, deep thoughts mind racing.

K. Gotti

Don't Miss This Plane

Don't miss this plane, dealing with the lames, that'll be insane, ain't you ready for a change, I'ma give you the real outside the game, and patience is a virtue, move to a place where 8:00 is the curfew; a better environment to raise the kids, refrigerator full so our stomachs never touch our ribs, and a private chef once or twice a week, that's a bonus plus a treat, that's the lifestyle living amongst the elite, gifts and new cars that's the way I greet, you name it I'ma claim it, I'm already hood famous, cause I make moves I'm winning even when I lose, cause I never quit, you're who I wanna be with, why not when you're hot, quarter to seven convertible drops, I follow in a CL six, baby we the shit, Tiny and Tip the family hustle, we doing it from the muscle, long distance; let the world witness, a dynasty like never before, different sides tuggawar, real deal not playing no games, Destiny Child say my name, and don't miss this plane.

K. Gotti

My Ex

When we met it was love at first sight, even though I was high as a kite, but that night was bright, at the bar, whoever thought we would've made it that far, a small child, the sex was wild, out that west, years ago you was considered the best, but that all changed, you stepped out your lane, and had three more babies by lames, never rode a bid with me that's a shame, I'm cool though I got a different mind frame, just wanted you to feel my pain, I brought you lots of gifts and flooded you in change, you ain't acting the same, copped you jackets and sneaks, kept your hair done every week, you loved me more at my peak, few steps away from hitting those streets, so keep playing musical beds under those sheets, I don't want you back like the Jackson Five, I came in with more then a starting five, Philly's most wanted Dead or Alive, your mad now cause you ain't keep your eye's on the prize, not a whole lot of truth mostly lies, I remember those days of making you cry, hanging up phones without saying good bye, a lot of what I did made you stress, it's not on me now your just my ex.

K. Gotti

Walk A Day In My Shoes

Disloyalty is worse than dying, that's why I break out when people start lying, I'm pass the tears so no more crying, brain like a bird it be flying, screaming for help, but everybody's denying, fighting two states, NY and PA, so damn if I ain't trying, you know the game is sour, when the lames think they thorough, I been to New York, only a few boroughs, even done time on Rikers Island C74, C73, C95, I had the streets on smash in 1995, Four blocks and ounces going for five, blew a lot money getting high, Syrup and Pills, plus weed, young wilding out in my teens, nobody looks past greed, spent my life in jail without raising my seeds, the struggle, no Mr. Deeds, gifts without the Christmas trees, all seasons, so I hustle hard that's the reason, asthma pump to stop the wheezing, I feel cold although my heart is still breathing, emergency room, shock treatment, party the whole week, not just the weekend, in the long run, that takes a toll, no matter what, I never fold, I'm older now, not old, loyal with a heart of gold, never catching me selling my soul, act like they solid, but be full of air holes, vote for the real dudes, we losing at the polls, but we still fight hard to win, even though we lose, walk a day in my shoes.

R. Gotti

A Mother's Pain

Mothers pain of losing a son, or even a daughter, she's hurt cause her child's life was cut shorter, no husband she's the only supporter, nerves shot, every night hearing shots, babies cry every time their loved ones dying, oldest child still in the system, it's hot in the kitchen, when will someone listen, visit's are overwhelming, stop snitching t-shirts, so no ones telling, so the drugs keep on selling, on every corner, can't call 911 or you're a gonner, blame it on poverty stricken, what do you do it was written, I swear God is my witness, no life insurance, blood pouring, can't afford a casket, so he's burned in a box, nowadays your not even safe from the cops, how many rapes do they got, and how many bodies did they drop, too many to count, check the headlines, they're winning the race on committing crimes, they're not even being charged even civilians have bodyguards, your kids can't find guidance, so they resort to violence, nothing but wasted talent, until there shown a better way, mom dukes visits her child's grave everyday, closed mouth cause she doesn't know what to say, on her knees praying for a better day, she knows the street code, a bruised heart and ached soul, and people say that's a shame, her grandchildren keep her sane, but you'll never understand a mother's pain.

K. Gotti

YOU'RE MY BEST FRIEND

You're more then my mother, you're my best friend, so much I wanna tell you, But don't know where to begin, been here since the beginning still hanging around in the end, held your boy down while he was locked in the pen, as well as my next of kin, you did your best to raise two boys to be men, so don't blame yourself, for me chasing the streets just to accumulate some wealth, I remember you working those extra hours, so we could have food on the table and electric and power, and you did it all alone, you should be proud that you own your own home, without relying on the bank for a loan, I don't drink and I feel like popping that Petrone, just to celebrate me coming home, and the fact we never strayed apart, you hold a special place in my heart, the will to win keeps me sharp, I'm only a son loving his mom they can't break that spark, one day we going leave this earth, I pray we be together the way we connected at birth, until then I'm holding us down like Poppa Smurf, no blue or red Christmas hat, just aiming for a home run since I'm up next to bat, did all my time mom and I ain't rat, so you should pat yourself on the back, for having a child that stands up, even with the pitfalls, rather big or small, I love all yaw, for moving out and sending ends, that's what happens when mom and son become best friends.

K. Gotti

Touchdown

Throw me your love like a football, I promise to catch it, like a wide receiver, working together we can be achievers, first down, aiming for a touchdown, fourth and goal, foul on the play its my heart you hold, I'm convinced sold, still calling plays like Andy Reid, cheerleader outfit white and green, we on the same team, yellow flag that's why they mad, I'm glad, penalty five yards back, stay on track, don't fear the contact, block I'm the quarter back, winning seven zip plus two sacks, lots of fans the stadium's packed, trying get to the top, without the illegal blocks, to many people on the field, I'm just keeping it real, horse collar, its all about a dollar, so hollar, stand by my side, not off sides, a few punt returns, show me your concerned, and your not just running in cause the money I earn, booth review, the call stands, I want you don't care about your man, another penalty for the face mask, celebrate fill up the glass, unnecessary roughness I'm smacking that ass, I'm the offense, you're on the other end defense, so represent 100 percent, new chick in my life, she trying be my wife, old girl trying, make a come back pass interference, look at her eyes they glaring, timeout, they want us on the outs, but it's a first down, still don't play your part when I'm not around, I'ma give you a two minute warning, so call me in the morning, red flag to challenge, it's all about balance, just don't drop the ball or step out of bounds, score touchdown.

K. Gotti

TALKING TO MYSELF

Told you not to help them, you shouldn't trust them, they aint have your back, now look where you at, why you sell those drugs, you gotta stay away from those plugs, they wasn't your friends, only thing they did is leech off your ends, you tried to make sure everybody got ahead, and they still left you for dead, no love even though you grew up from kids, why you overdose at seventeen, when you going stop running water and go green, you can do better without a team, ain't that the truth, been loyal since my youth, it's either me or my alter ego, lived my whole life illegal, without Malik and Jamal, I just wanted to ball, how you fall in the same ditch twice, I was just caught up in the life, crapped out a few times rolling the dice, big pie I only want a slice, greed that brings on envy, that ain't never been in me, treated a lot of folks equal, when I die there's no sequel, still got love for my people, no matter what, you gotta stand up, came a long way from getting high, and no more poverty so you're getting by, look at your status change, no drive to go back to the game you're in the entrepreneur lane, a helluva transition, you just gotta play your position, take the middle course, once married to the game now your divorced, no different from Benzino starting Hip Hop Weekly and leaving the source, now work on getting your book on the shelf, sorry yaw I'm just talking to myself.

K. Gotti

BIG MISTAKE

I admit I did you wrong, smashing all those chicks, I made you wifey my main bitch, but you still ain't do no riding my first bid, and I came home and gave you a second chance, I kept it strictly sex when you was trying romance, you even spoke on marriage, I couldn't see myself giving you a carrot, when you went from high class status to average, me having sex with your cousin justified you sleeping with my man, the one I grew up with my right hand, that shit hurt me like you was a witness against me taking the stand, still didn't understand the cross, but at the end of the game you still lost, and I can take it deeper, but I don't wanna feel like a revenge seeker, so next time stay in your place, when you decide to read my page or my space, I been down eleven years and I'm still winning the race, I ain't never track you down or invade your space, but you going see me or feel me soon so say your grace, and I ain't got nothing for you to eat but I'ma fill up Sobby's plate, Denzel Washington the great debate, bringing that up was a big mistake.

K. Gotti

Daddy's Home

Keep thinking I ain't going touch down, Daddy's home now, so mommy you can step down, I'm doing the opposite of what the haters want now, everybody gets a shot this my second round, get rich music so they can hear the sound, I'm discharged bound, same cat I ain't new in town, baby get comfortable I'm back, different flavor, we moving to a new location no neighbors, my old chick come back tell her Raider, no average leather all gator, black and white minks call it Oakland Raiders, we together now so I ain't gotta call you later, use your cell phone I'ma stick with the pager, I'm in my own league major, sorry for leaving you around all those strangers, aint trying get you in trouble, I need you girl your the pieces to my puzzle, we a team huddle, love it when we cuddle, late night watching the wire, your love has me inspired, you don't have to work anymore you're retired, and I'll pick up the slack of paying the bills, I'll do anything for you and that's for real, and no doubt good dudes catch raw deals, but I aint crying over the milk that spilled, that's water under the bridge I'm just playing the field, left you home like Kevin all alone, cheer up daddy's home.

K. Gotti

YOU'RE THE ONE

Look at your features, your a beautiful creature, you just need the right man that's going know how to treat you, love you when your up, take care of you when your down, if it didn't work the first time, try another round, whisper sweet nothings in your ear tell me how it sounds, you're a good catch not just a rebound, that's why you should know your worth, I don't know how life would be without you on this earth, we connected like two twins at birth, when it comes to you I'm gang related fighting over my turf, take you out to dinner shrimp and lobsters and have you for desert, watch you play dress up in your cheerleader skirt, trust me you're all I need so I aint gotta flirt, I'ma feel this way about you until I'm back in the dirt, six feet deep, boxed in underneath, X rated under the sheets, kiss you from your forehead down to your feet, you taste like sweet candy and I'm loving the treats, gift wrapped without the basket, glued together like Jay and Beyoncé we everlasting, do everything for you without asking, all in fun, if you're not my woman then I don't want none, cause baby your the one.

K. Gotti

Days Of Our Lives

My life is a story like day's of our lives, I ran the streets like cats with nine lives, a lot of games being played but at the end there's no prize, and that's word to the wise, tell me the truth. I can do without the lies, so many disloyal people in the world I just ask why, I hope to remain real to the day that I die, this is me no disguise, I'm on another chapter of my life since I got over the high, and its a beautiful feeling, specially when your arms can touch the ceiling, I done already laid the foundation, I put my pen to work like a certified mason, abortion is no different from masturbation, I followed my dreams without education, I can read and subtract I learned that in the basics, young at heart but its like my soul is ancient, I'm in overdrive shooting pass the patience, it's not only the words it's the intimidation, just give me my reward congratulations, save the applause that's just aggravation, cause you don't really mean it, be I'm thankful to be an author, poet, hustler and a genius, it makes me a triple threat, I'm repping for those who were put to rest, as well as the ones that's living, I can deal with the smiles but it's the hate that's hidden, but I'm gonna continue to hold my head high, as we go on in the days of our lives.

K. Gotti

HEARTBROKEN

Sorry if I broke your heart, sometimes I get caught up swimming with the sharks, if we couldn't finish why did we start, beware don't underestimate the bark, without you there's no spark, don't let the pride keep us apart, I would be lying if I said I didn't want you back, look at all those years you had my back, you inspired me to write, there's no wrong there's no right, this is our life, do anything to make it up, it's haters on both sides trying break us up, if it's a dream please baby wake me up, body going thru withdraws, I respect the stand and the fall even the statue of liberty stood tall, you wasn't there when I needed you, and you wasn't there when I called, it was love at first sight it was your beauty that I saw, I'm not going to sugar coat it I'ma give you the raw, I cared about you more then my dog, I'm human with a few flaws, it's like you want me to craw, but that's for babies, just wanted you to be my lady, this Love Jones is driving me crazy, and I hope you get it together and stop smoking, while I live with the fact you left me heartbroken.

K. Gotti

A Ride Or Die Chick

I need a ride or die chick, like Tiny move for Tip, and Chrissy move for Jim, hold you down in the pen, with you from the start, and still be there in the end, rather you did a year or ten, a few visits, flicks and exercise your pen, prepaid or the collect, not really chasing the checks, that'll come in due time, make you the star like your high school prom, trust me I'm inclined, the way Papoose rides for Remy Ma, I don't drink but have some Remy Ma, and a shot of coke, I don't need you for smuggling dope, just play your part if things blow up in smoke, with you in the trenches, play lookout when you on the block pitching, called for questioning never snitching, the way you move you gotta be feeling me, the haters be killing me, talking fly watching your every move like a spy, no matter what you do never lie, if I'm out of town I'll be back Jayz song cry, I'll keep you laced in all the latest fashion, you gotta a live cat mixed with thug passion, it's not a demand I'm just asking, the fakes are being exposed, and the real aint lasting, I want you ever lasting, million dollar checks we cashing, trips to Aspen, Hawaii in the summer, just take your pick, cause you a ride or die chick.

K. Gotti

Closer Than Neighbors

I enjoy walking and holding hands in the park, and sealing the deal making love after dark, no lights we bringing the sparks, I hold you dear to my heart, so don't break it, a few steps forward we gotta take it, as long as were together we going make it, real love we can't fake it, even if the odds aren't in our favor, still remain closer then neighbors, we on the same team no traders, Black and White Affair no waiters, middle finger up hi Haters, careful of those who might betray us, so many faces, do whatever to trade places, lets take our time remain patient, ain't nobody else hanging around waiting, everything is in our favor, the odds and ends, look how we grown from friends, stepping out of that zone, I'm prone and happy I'm not alone, I feel like a alcoholic stoned, focused when it comes to you mind never roams, opposite's do attract two tone, never hesitate to pick up the phone, no matter who calls, its all about us win lose or draw, when it comes to you I'm breaking the law, don't say a word I'm taking the fall, I'll protect you like a guard dog, to me you the best thing I ever saw, for you I'll continue to cater, as long as we stay closer then neighbors.

K. Gotti

Rough Pass

I had a rough pass, no molestation I'm talking no dad no cash, mom had to bust her ass, welfare cheese a loaf of bread we had to make it last, two sisters one brother arguing about who going take out the trash, cold nights had to save the gas, a few road blocks worse than a car crash, so I turned to the streets, started with 130 packs then I graduated to ounces in a few weeks, no broom but I call it a clean sweep, thousands a day I say the game is sweet, so I treated my siblings to a few outfits and some new sneaks, after that we made every greek, even hustle while the cops walk the beat, in front of the 3-2 center, spring, summer and winter, what can I say I'm a born winner, the hood is like killer whales, but I'm a pro swimmer, catch me on Facebook, my space and twitter, I see the jealousy that's why the taste buds are bitter, they can bow out cause I ain't never been a quitter, I suffered enough pain like Tina when Ike use to hit her, and the story is all so familiar, those in the same situation I feel ya, so don't let the setbacks kill ya, cause everything in life is a task, but all dirt aint guaranteed to grow grass, I just gave you a taste of my rough pass.

K. Gotti

Trust Me With Your Heart

Just place your heart in my hands, let me do the right thing like Spike Lee, and Ed Lover and Dre on who's the man, I got one hellava plan, green water and white sand, you gotta bad boy and you aint gotta make the band, you're a celebrity and I'm your number one fan, let me have your autograph, while I run your bubble bath, massage your feet and fill up your champagne glass, red rose petals, what I got in store will excite the devil, dry you off and lay you across the bed, I'ma explore your whole body and I'm starting from your head, down to your soft lips, I call it a thug passion French kiss, the rest is left for your imagination, enjoying each other's company is a celebration, you aint gotta wait once a year for valentine's, buy you gifts everyday to show you that your mine, your face reminds me of when the sun shines, stop thinking I'ma cross you that's a thin line, so don't hold me accountable for what those guys did in the pass, I'ma work extra hard to make it last, look how your situation changed now in your yard you can grow grass, and a private contractor to collect the trash, it's not even about the material, I'm cool chilling with you eating cereal, and watching a movie, real facts of life no tootie, this is how it starts, just need you to trust me with your heart.

K. Gotti

Lets Do It Big

Lets do it big, blow cash, shopping sprees at Dash, Mink Bra and Panties to cover your ass, spend it all no stash, bad chick Stacy Dash, held for detention only one in the class, flying private the only class, first class for those who trail last, port of Miami no pass, low rider jeans my broad showing her ass, Buffy the Body, Candy Apple Maserati, Cartier shotties, all white yacht call it Whitney and Bobby, Rolly's marked his and hers, Chin Chilla furs, just cause we on another level, foreign cars the right side is the pedal, balling outside the ghetto, you won the race I'm the medal, Bloomingdales Rodeo Drive why settle, boiling over pot kettle, NickelBack heavy metal, front row seats watching the fight in Vegas, the way we spending is so amazing, so lets do it big, us and the kids.

K. Gotti

Guilty Of Loving My Man

I'm up five o'clock in the morning, just to catch a bus, to visit my man in jail, and I don't think that's enough, I'm out here alone and things are rough, I guess the love is stronger than the lust, but he took care of me before he got caught up in the drug bust, and a few robberies, now I feel like he's robbing me, I know what I signed up for, I just be happy to see his face when he walks through the door, I pay the bills, on top of his Attorney fees for his appeal, I'm the mother and the father when the kids get ill, I call it being loyal not a bad ordeal, if I don't do it who else is going keep it real, death b-4 dishonor, he's the man of the family your honor, well he'll have a few years to ponder, cause he didn't care, so they want me out here on welfare, or struggling, haters are laughing cause they're use to seeing me bubbling, but they don't know I'm good and my children's stomachs aint rumbling, I'm just playing by the rules, riding with my man like I ain't got nothing to lose, and the ones that don't they're the fools, cause he'll be back home again, then we going cruise, or fly private jets or take a carnival cruise, back to business Hill Street Blues, I'll be waiting for you when you land, just guilty of loving my man.

K. Gotti

Charge It To The Game

Either the Benz or the coupe Deville, I'm playing the field, fresh out of jail, but I ain't carrying no steel, I got a bodyguard with two four pounds the size of Shaquille O'Neal, so cross the line your family gonna be reading the will, I'm riding hard like Macky from the shield, I write for fun was never searching for a deal, come through in that 760 ill, sober now no more popping those pills, team on standby like the Navy Seals, not from VA but got mad skills, living up on the hills, a bucket full of money Jack and Jill, I'm grinding for real, the flow is tight but the hand is ill, sick with no cure, cocaine is pure, no cut, it's the lames I'm trying to duck, and the gooses, yaw asses cooked, yaw on the lower level, I'm above the roof, my foot on your neck to keep you from running loose, Hype Williams I'm directing the shoot, top video vixens, call me Rudolph cause I'm ahead Blitzing, I'm still here even though yaw thought I was missing, I was washing dishes in the kitchen, staying in my own lane, don't care charge it to the game.

K. Gotti

So Sincere

Its my heart I spilled, and you question how I feel, like me loving you ain't real, you could feel it if you take down the shield, I'm comfortable better yet thrilled, that you got all my letters and cards, I'm in love with who you are, its not hard, you're a shining star, I want you no holds bar, your outer beauty is breathtaking, as well as your inner, open your legs let me enter, I'm missing you in the summer and the winter, never watched the pretender, different strokes for different folks, about you I'm going for broke, like how you laugh but its not a joke, I wanna see you happy even if what we got blows up in smoke, but it won't come from my end, I'ma play my part so we both win, I love all of you rather when your sad or when you grin, and I'm let the world know cause I can, willing to do whatever it takes, so you'll know the real from the fakes, I like pies but I prefer the cake, I want you there to celebrate my break, it's like give and take, and that's rare, but I'm so sincere.

K. Gotti

Thank Yaw All

Shots out to all my Facebook supporters, it's been a long time, now it's cut shorter, can't wait to hear may I take your order, that means I'm not locked up, I'm free now I done popped up, and I'ma show yaw the love yaw showed me, I'm one of a kind, they should've cloned me, my mom got her son back, the state no longer owns me, and we are altogether for better or for worse, talent aint only a gift it's a curse, and you're missed more in back of a hearse, I'm easy to find Google Search, just trying to pull it together before I leave this earth, bread winner I know my worth, free Gotti t-shirts, book signing and yaw all are invited, good food served so yaw should be excited, I appreciate yaw for reading my work and my man who typed it, this is only the beginning of our friendship, I pulled yaw in like kinship.

K. Gotti

If I Die Tonight

We never know when we going take our last breath, I'm still fighting but some days it feels like there's nothing left, a lot of checkers on the table but this is a game of chess, I'm just stock that the State Invest, trash everywhere but who going clean up the mess, I think I'm better but I'm just like all the rest, not knowing one day I'ma be put to rest, my mom said she's cool but deep down inside it's a lot of stress, I studied my whole life but still didn't past the test, and at times I just don't understand, robbed of my childhood I was forced to become a man, only to provide for my family, but all I hear is silence like a muzzle, what other choice did I have but to hustle, I feel cheated the cards wasn't shuffled, so I except the loss, eyes wide open still can't see the cross, still standing though a lot fell off, boxed in like Cleo set it off, a bucket full of tears, here today but can be gone next year, unexpected didn't have a chance to say goodbye to my peers, who cares if it ain't fair, you had your share, it's time to move on, after you're dead and gone, leaning over the casket as your family mourns, I'm at a standstill like a stillborn, and what about my pass, it caught up with my ass, not really scared of taking that flight, I just ask myself what if I died tonight.

K. Gotti

When I Roll Up

From eleven years to ten months, until I'll be able to take you out for brunch, for those that don't know that's breakfast and lunch, big family like the Brady bunch, that move when a nigga in the clutch, pay the whole tab the opposite of the Dutch, loyalty and trust, I aint ask for much, I'm dipping like a dope fiend, when they get that rush, its nothing but love I'm over the lust, we never argue or fuss, but if we do we always make up, never see signs of a break up, I need you like a shot of coffee when I wake up, I'm grinding baby trying to get my cake up, so I can show you the world, and everything in it, its sky's the limit, whatever you want you can get it, no price tag, throw it in the bag, don't know Fab, just trash bags, filled with paper, Ben and Grant, two brothers, I'm out in the open, never undercover, nothing to hide, over the water is where we reside, four car garage, we just doo dood on them Nicky Menage, forget about those other guys, the real is on the rise, the haters want us to sever ties, kill each other over the lies, they only love you when you die, so they use us as bait, I'm missing you baby can't help but wait, you can never do wrong in my eyes, loving the fact that you try, that's good enough cause its all about us, and I got the blue print to blow up, just live life gorgeous until I roll up.

K. Gotti

TOUGH LOVE

Got a whole lot of thanks to give, you been here my whole bid, riding with no breaks, you stand out amongst the real, opposite of the fakes, your so respected, even amongst the great, being pulled in different directions, just the fact that we're related is a blessing, trust me I've learned my lesson, you carried the burden for so long, like we both paid for my wrong, but we still standing like Monica, I know you heard that song, don't give up stay strong, because where there is a will there has to be a way, you deserve a basket full of gifts, without the holiday, for your loyalty to the family, I'ma make them pay, success that's the best way, don't stress out about being laid off, come with the company that'll be the payoff, we all got hustling in our veins, just different product, in different mind frames, big portrait put it in the frame, and let it hang off the wall, so it can be known that we move for a cause, even the ones that hated gotta love it, we did more than talk we done it, that's the best example, wait until I show so I can give them a sample, how kinfolk is suppose to stick together, and with unity everybody can do better, keep a tight team, so we all can live our dream, team stands for together everyone achieves more, only the real ride for sure, trust me it's alright to cry, I know you're still hurting from when you got the news that Lib died, and yaw were close, more than most, the show just started and your brother is the host, were gonna do it coast to coast, without the haters and bugs, this is brotherly tough love.

K. Gotti

Just Lost One

Far from being Jay but I just lost one, my Brother and my moms second son, everybody in the hood they die by the gun, but they don't know what they started cause the war just begun, and as long as I'm breathing I promise to make it even, and I'ma take care of your seeds like I'm the one who laid the semen, still can't picture you going its sorta like I'm dreaming, and I inherit your pain, I'm make they brains hang as low as Jibbs chain, and you don't never squash beef that's like changing the game, you got caught slipping, I wish I was there to catch the blood dripping, so on tilt you could've swore I was cripping, moms hurt the thought of putting you in the dirt, girl niggaz I'ma lift they skirt, the nerve of those jerks, and I'm ride all out until I join you or be cellies with Turt, real rap blood salutations to a thug, nothing but bullet proof love, you left behind two ladies, plus a new born baby, how can I forget about the fun we had in the eighties, and your memory will live on R.I.P. to you G, Kev . Massi, Butchie . Nert, Diddy and Vaughn, and I ain't forget about Billy, it's only a few real cats left and that's me, Ty, Fatta, Muff, and Hilly, and I heard about those fag's eating your flesh, until I run down on them and have 'em meeting with death, my goal is to get rich I can't settle for less, I got a big plate to feed, so it's only right I flood the blocks with bricks of cheese, not the rat kind, I prefer the pack kind, I'm make the block do a dime from midnight to sunshine, and my life will never be the same without you in it, and all I wanna do is get the cats who did it, and the pain will never be over, I wish I could bring you back like a Leprechaun with a four leaf clover, but I gotta stay strong so the family can lean on my shoulder, they done made the grind harder, they got your boy on the move like Stallone on get Carter, no picks and I won't stop until I put at least five of them in a ditch, like Joe Pesci on casino, I wish you was here so I could move the weed and you move the chino, (no holds bar), when they took your life they left the family scarred, and the only choice is revenge, when people see Mimi they look at her like yaw was Siamese twins, how about they got mommy working extra hard just to send me some ends, but I know I'm pay for my sins, I was mad when I heard you was riding around with those cowards, that lame they call Damon Bower, I heard he was ducking and dodging, better yet hiding, and cats tried to slander your name, broad niggaz trying gain fame, you wasn't Terri Woods but you was true to the game, you only had one friend and that was baby James, and the rest I don't care for, if they died tomorrow I wouldn't shed a tear for them, how do I explain to your kids that you died in the streets, yeah daddy did what he did so yaw could eat, and you always took care of Reema never missing a beat, I use to chase you off the block I ain't want you on J-street, I even took you shopping, had you wearing the same stuff I was rocking, and I wasn't Meiki Pfeifer but I was clocking, at the young age of 12, with dreams to prevail, when we got sick mom gave us ginger ale, hot soup, had to wear extra socks cause she couldn't afford boots, while all the other kids dressed up for Easter in TI sweat suits and Troops, hard times turned to hard crimes, state bids, chow halls long lines, late nights 55th and Pine, all for the love of the grind, you was a young bull still in your prime, and that's a shame cause even family members didn't want you to shine, they hit you nine times, but I'ma double that, and if I miss one I'm double back, and I'm a soldier so you know I'm moving in silence, Mayor Nutter wants to decrease but I'm increase the violence, plus we was blood brothers both with talent, and the fam they still missing you, even heard you had a few chicks at your funeral kissing you, while you lay dead in a casket, I swear I'm murder those bastards, its too late to realize they made a mistake, and the only ones I'm ducking is the Jakes, the game is over checkmate.

K. Gotti

Til Death Do Us Part

Until death do us apart, real love for you in my heart, no ring, we just young doing our thing, hold on tight to a string, don't let it break in half, thought out process can't move fast, a question we all gotta ask, did Kim and Kris do it for the cash, who cares, a lot of people still got their share, what about the parents still on welfare, and can't afford daycare, married twice, without the bouquet and rice, divorced twice, that's the ups and downs of life, long distance relationship, letters and phone cards no skype, with fame comes a price, not sure if your my enemy or my wife, there's no sleeping, or day dreaming, two kids mixed semen, everybody scheming, for what reason, greed and power, we made passionate love in the shower, connected on another level, heart beating heavy metal, prenup so a easy settle, part way's lonely days, where did we go wrong, loved your butt in those thongs, same old song, change the tune, bad boy no loon, you left your mark, it was suppose to be us til death do us apart.

K. Gotti

BONUS POEMS

Runaway Love

You ran off when I needed you the most, you was the butter to my toast, no marriage but we was close, not comedy central but still I felt like I was the head of the roast, in relationships time does tell, where did we go wrong I thought we was doing so swell, when we first met you was like a turtle I brought you out of the shell, and this whole situation stinks but I can't smell, you promised to stay until the end but I can't tell, it's like the world put you under a spell, ,the past is the past but I'm gonna dwell, and money can't buy love so I won't sell, welcome to part two of heart break hotel, I thought we would be locked up for life just minus the cell, a beautiful journey until you fell off the trail, being inpatient, How? when both of us could've been destined for greatness, how you going let 'em break this, the tight bond we once shared, I felt like the people under the stairs, two weeks turned into a few years, why didn't you tell me you was scared, I knew I was a different breed and my swag was rare, specially after being in the company of squares, I was in your presence a few times when you shedded those tears, keep acting like you don't care, I'm the realest dude you ever met and I ain't gotta swear, I was always a gentleman and thug, so do you runaway love.

K. Gotti

Dedicated To A Beautiful Woman

I dedicate this with a whole lot of respect, you was like family, as well as Ms. Peck; You watched us grow to men from kids on the steps . . . And we first met 1987 I was either ten or eleven, and how can I forget, these real life events, like on your porch swigging, I lost so many people that was close, sometimes I think, I'm dreaming . . . But it's the memories that I'm digging, each one has a whole lot of meaning, and I heard about those who took advantage of you stealing and scheming, When you was a nice lady, even treating my brother like he was your baby, I blame it on the drugs driving those people crazy . . . Plus I remember your husband which is your other half, I guess you can join him now in peace, since you both passed . . . I'll keep an eye out on your house and even water the grass, keep it clean and take out the trash . . . I dedicate this to a beautiful woman, you are a part of my future, as well as my past . . . It is your memory I gotta make last.

K. Gotti

INCARCERATED MIND

My eyes are open but I'm still sleeping, I'm talking to myself cause the strangers aint speaking, so I feel all alone, I'm reaching but my hand can't grab the phone, dialing the same numbers twice, what can I say this is what jail has done to my life, divorced I don't even know my wife, and my kids are all grown, voices in my head why daddy ain't home, lies told daddy's dead and gone, I heard that song, and the words are all wrong, can't say much I'm only a pawn, I'm underneath the grass waiting for someone to mow the lawn, so I can breathe, gotta use two hands when I sneeze, you don't know me don't judge me please, it's not me it's my mind under siege, grasping at the roots, false accusations that overshadows the truth, racism ain't going I'm still hanging from a noose, the courts are chasing me I'm unarmed but they still shoot, the judge doesn't slam the gavel he throws the boot, no hand on the bible just raising my right hand, outnumbered by the white and black klu klux klan, more people coming in they got a high demand, shot in the back the cops said I ran, messed up when your own kind takes the stand, after you picked twelve, doing anything to keep you from trying prevail, toe tag they said my body is for sale, and I gotta pay my fines, all because of my incarcerated mind.

K. Gotti

Faithful Lovers

Baby we don't keep secrets, I love when you put on that lingerie by Victoria Secret, and when you're at home sleeping, I'm out there getting money not creeping, it's like you're my destiny so I'm seeking. and when your in the shower call me a peeping Tom cause I'm peeking, never catch me making excuses, treat you with care and love not being abusive, your a major part of my life so don't consider yourself useless, I'ma be by your side if you lose your hair or become toothless, I like when you cook but tonight I'm taking you to Ruth Crist, afterwards go to a matinee, then to the crib and play hide and go seek like back in the day, just follow my footsteps let me show you the way, my intentions is not to lead you astray, or make you cry, look in my eyes they don't lie, you got everything you need and I'm the reason why, everybody else is calling it quits at least we try, I'm in it for the long hall never saying bye bye, I don't know about severing ties, this is us do or die, its been along time but look how we survived, the relationship started like a road trip never ending, I love you now the same way I did in the beginning, and when its cold buy you minks so you can cover, only we know what goes on underneath the covers, that's the reason we remain faithful lovers.

K. Gotti

So Personal

I can tell by the conversation that you got a lot on your mind, but you're a strong woman so you'll be fine, hold your head, wish I could put you to bed, and fix you some chicken noodle soup and some ginger ale, whatever it takes to get you well, kiss you on the forehead and inhale your smell, such a beautiful scent, I'm trying add to your life multiply plus the percent, make it where you aint never gotta pay rent, or come out your pocket, I'm going all out about you who going stop it, on this earth, somebody gotta hit it that's tattooed on my shirt, I'm trying come up like Curt, and I want us closer then Earnie and Bert, and whatever you going through I'll help you weather the storm, I'm just a man loving his woman it's the norm, I don't want you laying around all stressed out, I'ma do my thing shorty from Philly to down South, you should be thrilled that I'ma taking a new route, and when things get hard I'm not gonna bail out, or jump ship, you're who I wanna be with, you got the key but I'm the locksmith, and this ain't house party so we ain't gotta holler switch, we dancing to the same tune, it's a two seater car so we ain't making no room, that's for all the perpetrators, smile in your face but deep down inside they haters, but I'ma use role reversal, because it's all about you so personal.

K. Gotti

Last Of The Dying Breed

Its only a few cut from that cloth, before they snitch they'll rather blow they own head off, they can stand a win as well as a loss, always keeping it one hundred no sign of a cross, separating the workers from the boss, gas mask but still can sniff out the frauds, a whole different circle, dark glasses but far from Steve Erkel, they rep for the real, sending those J-Pays through the jails, and get well cards when you're ill, good dudes who caught raw deals, blindfolded chasing the mills, it took incarceration to exercise the skills. making a 360 U-turn, not one attorney we hire the firm, anything to get our team home, Mumi movement so you're not alone, disloyalty something we don't condone, that's a selfish trait, I'm allergic so I'm not biting the bait, came along way from making frivolous mistakes, still fighting for a break, I'm in the back row being blocked by the fakes, a lot of time behind the wall got set up by the jakes, that's something that's hard to erase, ducking the petty cats it's hard to escape, I wasn't touched as a child but I still feel like I was raped, by the system and old friends, mob related so no making amends, bias for committing the sins, left for dead that's what my status reads, what can I say last of the dying breed.

K. Gotti

HIDDEN AGENDAS
A NOVEL BY KAREEM TORAIN

www.ingramcontent.com/pod-product-compliance
Lightning Source LLC
Chambersburg PA
CBHW071117090426
42736CB00012B/1935

* 9 7 8 0 6 9 2 2 8 0 8 0 5 *

The Rapoetry of a Hustler is poetry at the highest level of stories told through poems based on true events in my life or someone else's life. Where you get to crawl inside the mind of a hustler BEST BELIEVE these poems are going to touch home. So allow my vision to take you on a journey that normal people dream of. Jay-Z said best poetry is rap. He spit it through the wire, I put it on paper! There's talent in everyone. Sometimes it has to be sought out, only because we under estimate our own selves. Even when the body is tied down the mind is free to roam. You can travel the world mentally and that's what I call thinking outside the box. We can't allow our minds or even our bodies to stay secluded. Freedom of speech means you're free to say what's on your mind. As well as what you're thinking at that moment. Story telling is an art that you perfect as life moves on. Words are as powerful as a gun but not so deadly.

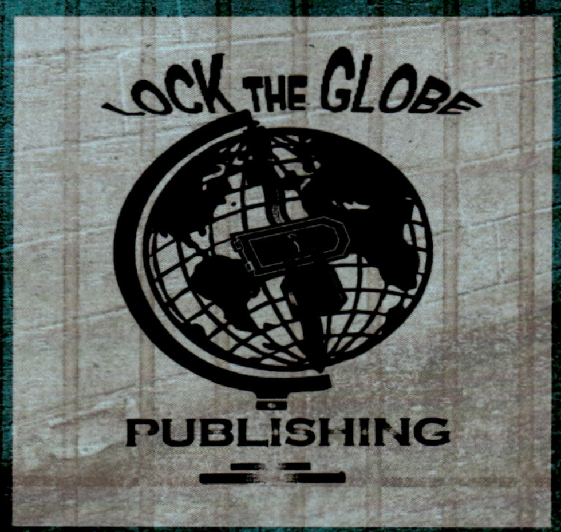

LOCK THE GLOBE PUBLISHING
P.O BOX 23639
PHILADELPHIA, PA 19143